Lead,
Follow,
or Get Out of
the Way

Proven Leadership Principles
for Youth Ministries in the 21st Century

Bret L. Allen

Lead, Follow, or Get Out of the Way

Proven Leadership Principles
for Youth Ministries in the 21st Century

TOOLZONE
4
LEADERS

Bret L. Allen
FOREWORD BY JEANNE MAYO

Published by:
ToolZone 4 Leaders
PO Box 276461
Sacramento, CA 95827

ISBN 0-9711064-0-1

Dedication

To Valerie . . .

My partner in ministry, this book is dedicated to you. Leadership is a lifetime ambition, an all-out effort to grow and improve. I want to thank you for joining me on this journey. I know that since we have decided to grow together we will never grow apart.

Acknowledgments

I owe a debt to my parents, Pastor Harley and Kaye Allen. Mom, thank you for believing in my dreams and in me. Thanks, Dad, for your example, your mentorship, and your leadership. But, most of all, thank you for all the times your office door was open for me. We were a great team! Thanks for the memories.

A very special thank-you to the Master's Commission interns at Calvary Temple in Concord. Your patience was noted and appreciated as I grew as a leader. The desire you demonstrated for personal growth set a standard for me to follow.

Thank you to Dr. John Maxwell for his influence in my life and ministry. Thank you for taking time to meet with Valerie and me and for praying with us.

Troy Jones, you are a true friend and a constant inspiration. Thank you for being one who believed in me and my ideas.

Finally, this book is dedicated to all those who strive for excellence and influence in leading this generation to our Lord Jesus.

Contents

Foreword

The famed Andrew Carnegie had powerful words inscribed on his tombstone: "Here lies a man who knew how to enlist the services of better men than himself."

What a powerful picture of the impact of true leadership. That is why Bret Allen's youth leadership manual, *Lead, Follow, or Get Out of the Way*, is such a vital asset for cutting-edge youth ministry. I commend it to you highly.

After three decades in youth ministry, I have observed countless people who fall short of their potential and destiny simply because they do not prioritize the training and mobilization of a leadership team around them. This generation of youth and young adults is eager to abandon themselves to a cause that is worthy of their passion. They need simply to have someone who has earned their respect and has strategically created a system to mobilize them. The day of the "Spiritual Lone Ranger" is far past.

It is a great thing when teenagers believe in their leaders. But it is even more exciting when a leader believes in his teenagers. Granted, leadership and mobilization come with their share of pain, risk, and price tags. But the rewards outweigh all the possible costs over and over again.

So find yourself a comfortable chair, grab some pizza and pop, and settle down with *Lead, Follow, or Get Out of the Way*. I promise you that it will be some of the most valuable time you have invested in your ministry. The manual is a great mix of pragmatic helps, changeable specifics, spiritual foundations, and inspiration. Even more exciting, it was written by a man who is in the trenches and "making it happen."

Thomas Edison said, "Show me a thoroughly satisfied man, and I will show you a failure." Congratulations on not being satisfied! After thirty years of youth ministry, I can honestly say that my most fulfilling times have all centered around some form of leadership training and discipling. You're in for a great ride!

Still passionate about molding history makers,

—JEANNE MAYO
Cross Current Youth and
Young Adult Ministries
Rockford, IL

Preface

Thank you for taking the time to pick up this manual on leadership. It speaks well of you. It means that you are willing to invest in yourself, your resources, and your time on your single most needed trait: leadership. The reason I wrote this manual is twofold:

First of all, I want to provide a tool to challenge your mindset about youth ministry. I want you to look at your youth and their potential in a new light. Some of my statements are pointed and a little strong; that is intentional, because I am passionate about the subject.

Secondly, I want to share in a simple format the things that I have learned that caused my youth ministry to grow and touch teens for Christ.

It is my hope that you will find a fresh look at youth ministry. I hope this book proves to be a tool of encouragement and blessing to you and those you lead. Youth pastor, we need you! Lead well.

chapter 1

What Is Leadership?

This is an age-old question. This question must be answered, understood, and lived if we are going to touch our youth culture.

In 1997 my wife and I traveled to Orlando, Florida, to hear Dr. John Maxwell speak at his leadership conference. We were by far the youngest couple there, so we decided to quietly blend into the crowd and do nothing to draw additional attention to ourselves. In short, the experienced crowd of pastors who were attending this conference intimidated us. At one of the breaks a pastor from the East Coast confronted me.

"Where are you from?" he asked.

"We are from the San Francisco area."

"Oh, from California. I see. How big is the church you pastor?"

"I am not a senior pastor. I am a youth pastor," I said.

"A youth pastor?! Why in the world does a youth pastor need to attend a leadership conference? What possible leadership needs could you have?"

Unfortunately, this attitude is not limited to a few people on the East Coast. This attitude about youth ministry and leadership has been accepted and acted on by dozens and dozens of ministries. Youth ministry is totally dependant upon strong leadership. Nothing in life exceeds its level of leadership. Leadership sets the pace. If a leader sets a low standard of conduct, everything will settle beneath that level of expectation. But if leadership sets a high standard, everything will rise to that level. This makes leadership the single most important commodity in any ministry. Now, I can already hear the objections. What about prayer? What about evangelism? What about preaching and counseling? What about taking large offerings? Without strong leadership none of those things can be successful. Strong leaders in charge of the decision-making process are the only ones who can make those things produce good fruit.

Even if they were somehow successful, their product wouldn't be handled correctly without strong leaders in charge. Leadership is what encourages people to pray. Leadership equips people to evangelize. Leadership causes them to listen to your sermon. Leadership gives them the confidence to give obediently to the work of the Lord. Everything in ministry rises and falls on leadership. Leadership, then, quickly becomes the single commodity without which you can't survive. Leadership is the biggest determining factor in your ministry.

A youth pastor?! Why in the world does a youth pastor need to attend a leadership conference?

I am sick to death of seeing vibrant ministries, churches, and programs killed because of poor leadership. How many churches need to go bankrupt? How many youth ministries need to fail? How many projects need to end in embarrassment until we discover the fact that we are dependant upon godly leadership for success? Vision is vital. Great preaching, a must. Counseling for the hurt and lost is a valuable asset. But none of these will ever replace your need to lead. It puzzles me why

Everything in ministry rises and falls on leadership

we spend so much time, interest, and effort developing these lesser skills while ignoring leadership development in our lives. Why do I as a youth pastor need leadership development in my life? Because I want to succeed! With this basis, the question, "What is leadership?" is vitally important. But of greater importance is how we answer it, so we can determine how and why we lead.

In an effort to define leadership, let's start by stating some things that leadership is not.

LEADERSHIP IS NOT

- A power trip
- That you are always right
- An indication that you are the only one with good ideas
- Something you should take lightly
- A position or title
- Something that is given to you. (You earn it)
- An inborn quality. (It's a developed skill)
- Something you can fake
- Something that can be achieved through shortcuts

Leadership takes time. There is no substitute.

Leadership is defined by one word: *influence*. Leadership, true leadership, is not determined by gray hair or the number of years lived or money given to the church. Rather, leadership is the influence an individual has with other people. Influencers come in all shapes, sizes, and ages.

Leadership is not position, neither is it title. If you think for one minute that people will follow you because of your title, wake up. We live in a day and age when the average teen has rebellion problems in their life. They come ready to resist and fight against organized leadership. When you announce your title or position to them, they don't care. It will be that way the rest of your life in ministry.

Each year, when new interns come to work for me, it is interesting to watch them struggle with this concept, that leadership is not determined by one's position or title. Without fail, one of my interns will give a directive to a group of our youth. Some of the time the order falls flat on the ground. I cringe inside when I hear them say, "You have to listen to me—I'm in leadership!" Our world cares very little about the nameplate on your office door. The person who tries to lead by position is in serious trouble, because very few will ever follow that person. If you think your title will impress today's teens or their parents, then you are in for frustration and disappointment. Check this philosophy out by asking your leadership team to take the following test.

Influence Test

"In 30 seconds, please write down five sermon titles from the messages you've heard me preach in the past year."

1.
2.
3.
4.
5.

"In 30 seconds, please write down the top three people who have influenced your life."

1.
2.
3.

I have administered this test dozens of times within my ministry. The results are always the same. The results always humble me. The results always remind me of what is really important in ministry. Never once has a person been able to remember five sermon titles from the past year. Yet every person is able to remember the people who have influenced their lives. What does this prove? People impact people. Leadership is influence!

chapter 2

But You're Only 16

Don't let anyone look down on you because you are young, but set an example for the believers in speech, in life, in love, in faith, and in purity. (1 Timothy 4:12)

Within this scripture lies the very heart of youth ministry. This passage must be understood and embraced in order for a young person's life to change into a productive member of the body of Christ. These words, when understood, will light a passion that cannot be extinguished. It will provide purpose that will ensure you are never wondering what to do or why you are doing it. It will provide focus and singleness in your mindset concerning youth ministry. As youth ministers we need to avoid the pitfall that America, in both the secular and Christian arenas, has fallen into. That pitfall is to overlook the significance, the irreplaceable value of teenagers. Almost everything spoken or written in the secular world, as it pertains to teenagers, is negative. Gangs, drugs, sex, abortions, violence at school, depression, and suicide get all the press headlines. There never seems to be enough ink leftover to print stories about the incredible value of America's greatest resource.

The American press has labeled them.*

- "The Doofus Generation", *The Washington Post*
- "The Tuned Out Generation", *Time Magazine*
- "A Generation of Animals", *The Washington Post*
- "The Numb Generation", *The New York Times*
- "The Blank Generation", *San Francisco Examiner*
- "The Unromantic Generation", *The New York Times*

Howe and Strauss in an effort to define this generation have called them "thirteen," because they are the thirteenth generation born since the signing of the constitution of the United States.

The church, for the most part, has followed suit with this mindset. Youth ministry is seen as a necessary evil. It is viewed with disgust and resentment as money is spent on "those kids." I once worked in a church that had a very weak youth group when I joined the church staff. My efforts there always seemed to be an uphill battle. I couldn't figure out why there was so much resistance to the growth and vitality of our youth group. I was told by one of the old saints that a pastor several years earlier had stood in the pulpit and made the following comments about the youth in that church: "This church is not for teenagers. If you want a youth group, go to another church. We have nothing here for teens." Other churches simply fold their youth ministries because it requires too much effort and expense. With mindsets, vision, and scriptural understanding like that, no wonder Satan has a bigger youth group than we do!

---

* *The Next Generation*, Gary Zustiak (Joplin, MO: College Press Publishing, 1996) p. 21.

Youth ministry is seen as an entry-level position, a trial ground to prepare young men and women for "real" ministry opportunities. Recently in my home church, where I have been the youth pastor since 1993, I was asked a question that exemplifies the attitude I am discussing. A dear old saint I love and respect approached me after a Sunday night service in which I spoke. In an effort to compliment me she said, "That was very good. When are you going to become a real pastor?" I thanked her for the compliment and walked away saddened by the fact that we in the church don't see youth ministry as a position filled by real pastors. In fact, some churches and their pastors see youth ministry as nothing more than a babysitting service. I am offended by that mindset! That attitude taints the view of the entire church toward the value of the youth ministry and its leadership.

Youth ministry is the high calling! Youth are more important than a clean-up crew for the church picnic, even more significant than a workforce to set up chairs for the other "real" ministries. I believe in servanthood, but I just don't believe that those are the most significant purposes for our church youth ministry. I value the ministry that God has called me to. I see significance in what I do. I am passionate about the teens I minister to. I am desperate to reach the ones who don't know Christ. I understand that the body of Christ is dependant upon the youth portion of our congregations to be complete. Scripture makes it clear that the youth is to set an example for the believers to follow in five major areas of conduct. Youth pastor, your ministry is very significant! Look further at these five areas in which you are called to equip your teens to be examples for the believers.

1. In Word

The conversations and speech patterns of a Christian young person should be exemplary, truthful, gracious, and pure. Our speech is incredibly important to us as Christians. It is one of the first things people will notice that sets us apart from the rest of this world. Our speech has the power to *compel* or *repel* people as soon as we begin talking. No wonder so many Christian teens have problems with their speech, like sarcasm, crude joking, threats, swearing, and gossiping. These problems cover the landscape of teen culture. Satan understands that each of these areas has the power to destroy a testimony and hurt the ability for a young person to set an example for the believers.

In our ministry in Concord, California, I teach teens three important lessons regarding their speech and how they use their words. These three areas are designed to create awareness of how important healthy and godly speech patterns are for Christians. Here are those three lessons and the scriptural references we use in each lesson.

WE MUST TAME OUR TONGUES

> We all stumble in many ways. If anyone is never at fault in what he says, he is a perfect man, able to keep his whole body in check. When we put bits into the mouths of horses to make them obey us, we can turn the whole animal. . . . Likewise the tongue is a small part of the body, but it makes great boasts. . . . It corrupts the whole person, sets the whole course of his life on fire, and is itself set on fire by hell. All kinds of animals, birds, reptiles, and creatures of the seas are being tamed by man, but no man can tame the tongue. It is a restless evil, full of deadly poison. With the tongue we praise our Lord and Father, and with it we curse men, who have been made in God's likeness. Out of the same mouth come praise and cursing. My brothers, this should not be. (James 3:2–3, 5–10)

Our tongues have the ability to create great trouble for us. Trying to control the tongue in our own power is futile. As capable as man is with his intellect and abilities, the tongue can never be tamed by a man. The only way we can bring our tongue under control is by God helping us in our effort. Once our tongue is under control, we are under control. We must tame our tongues if we are ever to be under God's control and useful for His kingdom.

THE WORDS YOU USE REVEAL YOUR HEART

> . . . For out of the overflow of the heart the mouth speaks. The good man brings good things out of the good stored up in him, and the evil man brings evil things out of the evil stored up in him. But I tell you that men will be judged for every careless word they have spoken. For by your words you will be acquitted, and by your words you will be condemned. (Matthew 12:34*b*–37)

This is an incredible truth. The things that come from our mouths are the products of what is in our hearts. Our words are an open invitation for others to look and see the condition of our spiritual man. Many times a young person will swear in my presence and simply say, "Sorry, Pastor Bret, I slipped."

My response is always the same, "You didn't slip. You revealed who you really are." It is impossible for young people to take their place as examples in the area of speech if they are constantly slipping. Those slips mean that issues of the heart need to be addressed.

OUR SPEECH MUST BE FULL OF GRACE

> Let your conversation be always full of grace, seasoned with salt, so that you may know how to answer everyone. (Colossians 4:6)

The third area of speech is the fact that God expects your speech to be a blessing to others. Earlier, we looked at a scripture that compared the tongue to a flame. Flames are not bad if they are controlled in my living room fireplace. In that setting, the flames are a blessing. The same is true with the tongue. It isn't enough to strive just to control our tongue; it must become a *blessing* to others. Our speech should always be filled with grace. And why should it be seasoned with salt? Salt is an agent that preserves. Our speech should be a preserving agent for those around us. Anybody can use their speech to tear people down. Anybody can gossip. It doesn't take a special gift to slander or malign another. It takes a special person, an example, to use his or her speech wisely in encouragement, truth, and peace.

Our youth must tackle the issue of speech if they are to set an example for the believers. Nothing is as detrimental to a witness as a tongue that is out of control. Likewise, nothing is as attractive as a young person who builds and uplifts those around him with his words. Teach them to set examples in their speech.

2. In Life

How you live your life is proof of what you say. Your life is being watched at all times by someone. Your life is preaching a sermon. And yes, it is the only gospel message some will ever hear. Scripture calls us to a high level in our daily lives.

> But just as he who called you is holy, so be holy in all you do; for it is written: be holy for I am holy. (1 Peter 1:15–16)

> Who is wise and understanding among you? Let him show it by his good life, by deeds done in humility that comes from wisdom. (James 3:13)

> Remember your leaders, who spoke the word of God to you. Consider the outcome of their way of life and imitate their faith. (Hebrews 13:7)

Follow my example as I follow the example of Christ.
(1 Corinthians 11:1)

These are important scriptures on how our lives are to be conducted. Our teens must understand that having their speech under control is only the first step. It is essential that their lifestyle match what they are saying. If they talk the talk, they must walk the walk. Nothing forms a more powerful testimony than a teen who is living a spirit-controlled lifestyle. Teenagers are known for living life on the edge and pushing the envelope. They are also known for not always exercising a high level of good judgment. But it makes an incredible impact on the body of believers when teens begin to honor God in their relationships, honor authority, and use their money and free time wisely.

One of the highlights of my ministry is having teens share testimonies during Sunday evening services. The teens are so honest and open. Their perspectives are fresh and unrehearsed. Their communication skills are not professional, but their messages always seem to hit home. Without fail, the adult members of our church line up to thank and encourage the young people who share what God is doing in their lives. I stand back with a sense of pride and accomplishment, knowing that the believers in our assembly are being impacted and encouraged to follow the examples set by teenagers. Teach your youth so they can set an example for believers to follow.

3. In Love

Young people need to learn to sacrifice themselves for others. That is the very heart of ministry. It is foundational in all we believe. Love must be at the center of who we are and everything we do. Without love we are nothing according to 1 Corinthians 13. Love is an element that our teens must quickly understand and model in their daily lives. This love must be modeled not only in our church, but also to the world that we live in.

This assignment of teaching teens to love is not as easy as it sounds. There are some built-in hurdles and obstacles. The teens that fill our youth ministries live in a world that is void of love. They live in a world where *love* is a word that is used as leverage to get something. The concept of true love is being lost. It has been successfully twisted and perverted into many things, like lust, usury, and self-gratification. It is incredible to think of all the ugliness that goes on in the name of love. Teens are fed rebellion, wholesale hatred, violence, and self-indulgence at every corner. Satan has certainly done a masterful job of warping the concept of love for this generation by allowing them to grow up without an accurate picture of love. They don't know what it means to love and be loved. Homes and families, which were designed by God to provide love, have been shredded and, in some cases, totally destroyed. The family unit has been so attacked that we are having difficulty even defining what a family is. To modern America, two lesbians and a goldfish could constitute a family unit! Where is the love? How are teens ever going to learn about love so that they can set an example for the believers?

That is where you come in, youth pastor. Teens must be *shown* and then *taught* the truth of love. There is no way a teen will ever be able to minister love, display love, or exemplify love until they are loved. Bottom line: Your teens need you to love them. Love to a teen doesn't come in the form of gifts, kind words, or a heart-warming sermon. To a teenager, love is communicated in time spent and investment made in their lives. It will take investment for this generation to learn what love is. Investment always means greater involvement. Once we love them, they learn about God's love. Once they experience

God's love, then they are able to set a powerful example of love for the believers in the body of Christ.

4. In Faith

Teenagers are militant. They just seem to come built that way. Even non-Christian teens are ready to support and fight for a cause, right a wrong, or try to free Tibet. Teenagers come equipped with an extremist mindset. They are willing to go and do. Risk is fun and exciting, never a fearful experience. Teenagers seem to have a zest and zeal when it comes to living. Teens hate to be bored. They are always ready to try a new thing or experience a new activity. These traits are what make teenagers powerful in the area of faith. Teens need to do more than sit in a youth room, singing cute little songs. They need to go into the street and witness. They need to learn dramas and then perform them for a crowd of people in an urban setting. Teens are the members of the church who get excited about giving out sack lunches to homeless people in the community. Teens seem to have a kamikaze mentality that allows them to excel in their faith relationship with God.

Recently I was watching the evening news. I found myself captivated by a series of events taking place half a world away. There was a small group of terrorists holding hostage a 747 jet full of passengers. One of the terrorists stood on the wing of the airplane with a ski mask over his face. In his hands he held an AK-47 automatic rifle. He stood confidently, defiant, as the news cameras filmed him. The reporter's voice was filled with fear as he reported the story. But the terrorist, on the other hand, displayed no fear at all. I said to myself, *That is what the church of today is missing: people who are so sold out for the cause of seeing the world changed that they will do whatever it takes, against whatever odds, to see their purpose achieved.*

Now please don't misunderstand me. I do not support violence; I hate it. I detest terrorism. But I am intrigued with the dedication and willingness to give all for the cause. Teenagers are militant. They love to be a part of something that is making a difference. Teens are ready to pour their lives into something they can believe in. All they need is the opportunity. That is where you come in. Youth pastor, this is going to demand that you get out of your office and get involved in the world around you. Your teens will never be militant for the cause of Christ unless you lead the way. For this reason, our youth ministry here in Concord, California, maintains a standard that 80 percent of our time, effort, and resources are spent on projects outside our church. Outreach is important to us because that is how we contact the lost and provide an opportunity for teens to be a part of something that makes a difference. We are also very active on eighteen campuses in our area. We are concerned about the condition of the public school system. For that reason we are active in our approach to take the gospel of Jesus Christ on campus. In addition, we take a mission trip every summer to another country. This allows teens to work, sacrifice, and save for the expressed purpose of making a difference in another part of the world. Our churches need to see militant teens who are willing to go anywhere, say anything, do anything, and sacrifice for their faith.

The Christian lifestyle is a war. We are in battle everyday. Our war is against spiritual forces that exist to destroy this generation. This war will never be won by people who are complacent in their church pews, showing more concern for their own comfort and ease than they do for people who are going to hell. That is why believers need to see teenagers set an example in the area of faith. Believers need to see the faith of militant teens who are sold out to doing all they can to love Jesus in real, practical, and effective ways.

5. In Purity

Purity is an old-fashioned concept. Just the mention of the word invokes feelings of anger and disdain. The word *purity* has almost lost any point of reference in our self-indulgent world. As a refresher, allow me to give you Webster's definition for this antiquated word: "Freedom from evil or sin, innocence, chastity" (*Webster's New Collegiate Dictionary*, 1977).

Examples of purity are very rare in a world of moral filth, situational ethics, and degeneration. Purity goes beyond sexual chastity; it includes business integrity, a wholesome thought life, and pure motives.

- Purity: The trait that is representative of a bride without spot or wrinkle
- Purity: A standard that holds regardless of the changing times, morals, norms of society
- Purity: The characteristic demanding nothing less than total dedication of one's lifestyle
- Purity: A trait that seems to have gone out of fashion in our world but is still seen as a requirement for us as Christians

For it is written: "Be holy because I am holy." (1 Peter 1:16)

. . . You ought to live holy and godly lives as you look forward to the day of God and speed its coming. (2 Peter 3:11–12)

But rather he must be hospitable, one who loves what is good, who is self-controlled, upright, holy, and disciplined. (Titus 1:8)

This purity includes sexual chastity, business dealings, thought lives, and a pure heart. If your heart is pure, your actions will also be pure. Just like Joseph faced temptation, our youth must stand strong and set an example in the area of purity for the believers.

I believe that this generation will measure up to the expectations set for it. The problem is that the expectations that are being set are very low and godless. Recently, I was driving through some old neighborhoods with an ex-gang member who attends my youth ministry. As I drove, he explained how his life had degenerated in this neighborhood. He said, "I was immoral with girls, did drugs, and I was violent, because that was who people expected me to be." Those words hit me like a sledgehammer. People expected that? Incredible.

One day, Peter was washing out his nets and Jesus arrived at the water's edge and said, "Follow me and I will make you fishers of men" (Mark 1:16–17). Peter left his nets and followed Christ. Nobody can convince me that Peter understood what Christ had called him to do. Peter had no idea what it meant to fish for men. But that is exactly what Peter became: a fisher of men. And the day he was martyred he had met the expectation Jesus had set for him. The same is true today. Our youth will rise to the expectations we set for them. Just like my young friend who lived with the gangs, he became what they expected.

I want to be the one to set the expectation for this generation! I plan to love them and set the expectations so high that they can be an example for the believers in word, in life, in love, in faith, and in purity.

This youth generation is incredible. They have abilities like no other generation before. Youth bring great things to life. They are dreamers. They have a unique strength. They are risk-takers. They have a passion for life. They were not called to slide by, or to be the church of tomorrow. They were called to set an example for the believers in five major areas. Lead them, teach them, and train them so they can do what God has called them to do.

chapter 3

Prepare Them, Be Obedient, and Succeed

It was he who gave some to be apostles, some to be prophets, some to be evangelists, and some to be pastors and teachers, to prepare God's people for works of service, so that the body of Christ may be built up until we all reach unity in the faith and in the knowledge of the Son of God and become mature, attaining to the whole measure of the fullness of Christ. Then we will no longer be infants, tossed back and forth by the waves, and blown here and there by every wind of teaching and by the cunning craftiness of men in their deceitful scheming. Instead, speaking the truth in love, we will in all things grow up into him who is the Head, that is, Christ. From him the whole body, joined and held together by every supporting ligament, grows and builds itself up in love, as each part does its work. (Ephesians 4:11–16)

What a scripture! This passage holds within it some great promises and some definite direction for successful youth ministry. Leadership will determine its own level of effectiveness or failure by how it handles the principle in this passage. This scripture encourages us to see the value in the teens we are called to lead. The principle here is to train the saints, including teens, to do the work of the ministry.

Such an idea flies in direct opposition to an entertainment youth ministry model. Pizza parties and hayrides are fun but have no spiritual impact on the lost. I state on a regular basis from my platform, "I am not an entertainer. I am not here to please you or to make you like me, but to challenge you. If I were an entertainer I would be a big brown bear who rides a unicycle or juggles. I am a man of God with a passion to see your life changed." I believe in a direct approach with my teens because they can handle it and they appreciate the honesty. They know I care about their eternal well-being. At the helm of an entertainment-based organization is usually an individual, a youth leader, who is trying to do it all. From start to finish, he/she single-handedly runs every aspect of the ministry: the services, activities, outreaches, planning, setup, and cleanup—the entire youth ministry! My friend, that is disobedient to Scripture. People who direct youth ministry in this manner are meeting a selfish need for power or control. Youth ministry doesn't exist to meet the needs of a leader, but to meet the needs of youth in a community. Too many youth pastors determine their worth by how busy they are, but busyness doesn't necessarily imply effectiveness or obedience. Too often we think that we have to do it all or people won't see the need for our position.

I remember the day I was set free from this mindset. I was proud of my eighty-hour workweek. I bragged about how I sacrificed family for ministry. I saw value in working all night while my family slept. I was working very hard to please God. I felt that if I worked harder, God would love me more. I was desperate for God's approval.

One night, as I worked in my home, my five-year-old son, Ryan, entered my office and interrupted my sermon preparation. He was clutching in his small hands his latest work of art: a purple dinosaur he had drawn, cut out, and painted. My office wall was already filled with such dinosaurs. I had every size, shape, and color of dinosaur one could possibly imagine. Ryan proudly announced, "Here, Dad. I made this for you."

Youth ministry doesn't exist to have your needs met, but for you to meet the needs of the youth in your community.

I thanked him, took the dinosaur, and began feverishly looking for an empty space on my wall to hang the masterpiece. After I hung it up, I said, "Hey, jump up on my lap, give me a hug, and spend some time with ol' Dad." My son pulled away and announced that he was too busy. "Too busy? You're only five years old!"

His response hit me like a ton of bricks. "I have to go make more dinosaurs, Dad, because that is what makes you happy with me." Tears filled my eyes as he left my office and ran down the hallway to his bedroom.

As I sat in silence, God spoke to my heart, *Bret, that is how you treat me. You are so busy doing work for me that you have no time for me. You think your busyness makes me love you. Please know that I didn't hire you—I adopted you.* That night my ministry changed. I quit trying to impress men, but more importantly, I quit trying to impress and win the favor of God. I quit basing my value and significance on what I produced.

Let me say to you: God didn't hire you; he adopted you! You are far more valuable than what you produce.

You can rest secure in the fact that no matter how much you work, no matter how much you do, God won't love you any more or less than He does right now. Perfect unconditional love can't be earned or improved upon. Just like dinosaurs had nothing to do with my son's value, so, too, the hours you work have nothing to do with your significance. Once you understand this, you are free to train and release the saints to do the work of ministry, knowing that their success isn't a threat to your position, but rather the fulfillment of God's promise to you.

You are to train the *saints* to do the ministry. This concept totally challenges the thinking of some of you. Try the following self-test.

Self-Test

Place an *x* next to each item that you routinely handle in your ministry.

- ❑ Set up youth room
- ❑ Print bulletins and flyers
- ❑ Lead worship
- ❑ Welcome visitors
- ❑ Make announcements
- ❑ Preach the sermon
- ❑ Lead new converts to Christ
- ❑ Lead all the youth activities
- ❑ Call absent members
- ❑ Conduct visitation

If you marked three or more of the above items, you are doing too much. Stop doing, start training, and allow the saints to do the work.

Many choose to ignore this concept by making excuses for why it doesn't apply to them. Their church is too small, too big, too poor, too wealthy, in the inner city, in the country, their senior pastor stifles them, the senior pastor gives too much freedom. On and on it goes, but the fact doesn't change: You are called to equip saints to do the work of the ministry. As a youth leader, prepare youth to do the work of the ministry.

It isn't enough to see youth as examples, as discussed in the last chapter. It isn't enough to acknowledge their value. *Believe* in that value and release them into real ministry opportunities. Only when they are released to do real work is this scripture fulfilled.

Look at the promises listed in Ephesians 4:11–16.

1. The body of Christ is built up (v.12)
2. Unity is reached (v. 13)
3. Maturity happens (v. 13)
4. The fullness of Christ is attained (v. 13)
5. We will no longer be infants (v. 14)
6. Speaking the truth in love (v. 15)
7. Each part does its work (v. 16)

This is what we are all working toward. These are the goals we have. These seven things are sought after by thousands of youth ministries across the United States. And these are what transform teens into productive members of the body of Christ. These are the things that impact and change communities.

Incredible promises, but like every promise, there is a requirement to be fulfilled. You and I must train and release our young saints into ministry. There are four things you must remember when you are training the saints to do the work of ministry.

1. See the Value of Youth

A personal goal for every youth pastor is to recognize the value of the teens in his or her ministry. People have value just because God created them, and God has invested talent and promise into each one. They are valuable because Christ chose to die for those individuals. Their value is without measure. Our job is to identify their value. Time, effort, and interest are required, but you will know how and where to invest into a young life.

My leadership team and I accomplish this through an activity we learned from veteran youth leader Jeanne Mayo, called "frog kissing." In the old fairy tales, wicked witches turn handsome princes into ugly frogs. They are held captive in that state until the beautiful princess comes and releases them from bondage with the kiss of true love.

The same is true in the world of youth ministry. Satan traps beautiful young people in bondage. Love frees them to be all they intended to be. These students enter our youth ministries and make up the fringe section of the youth group. For this reason, we kiss the frogs. My interns and I each find a young person on the fringe of our youth ministry and take him or her out for an hour-long lunch meeting to simply love that young person. We speak value into their lives and reveal the potential they have to serve God. As we spend time with teens, we begin to identify their unique qualities. This last year, my staff and I kissed over three hundred frogs! Dozens and dozens of princes are being set free. Find their value!

People have value just because they exist.

2. Invest Yourself in Others

To me, this is the very heart of youth ministry: pouring myself into others. Giving my time, money, energy, experiences, and love to teenagers. The reason? So that their lives will produce effective ministry—and our world will be won to Christ. I believe the best way to show this is to present the before and after of a few young "frogs" I have been privileged to "kiss."

BEN JOHNSON

Before

Ben was every youth pastor's nightmare. He was raised in a Christian home and knew all the pat answers. The problem was that he didn't believe any of them. Ben was a troublemaker. He frequently sat in the back row in my youth ministry and provided comic relief for those around him. Ben was my greatest frustration when I first came to pastor Crossfire in Concord. One night, on my way home from a youth group meeting I was literally screaming in my car from the frustration that Ben had caused that night. I stopped the car. I just wanted to think about Ben without crashing my car and killing myself. That's when it dawned on me that Ben had leadership qualities. People were responding to his influence. The problem was that I had never entrusted anything to him. I decided that night to give Ben a chance in ministry.

The next day, I had a meeting with Ben and offered him a position on our brick-breaking, phonebook-tearing, power team called CREW Power. He was excited and quickly accepted. My next job was more difficult: informing the team about our newest member. At a team meeting, I made my announcement. The proclamation was met with stiff resistance. The team sided against me. "If you bring Ben on this team, we will all quit!"

It was time to believe in Ben. I said, "OK. Then I will start this team all over with just Ben and me. Hand in your uniforms tomorrow." The next day came and went, and everybody stayed on the team.

After

Within six months, Ben Johnson was on fire for God, filled with the Holy Spirit, and leading the CREW Power team on all their outreaches, both foreign and domestic. Ben ended up serving on Master's Commission for two full years, where he touched countless lives of young people. After Ben left my youth ministry he went to work in the district office for the Northern California and Nevada Assemblies of God. Ben is currently serving as the Speed the Light representative for Northern California and Nevada. I keep in touch with Ben frequently. I love hearing about the youth groups he visits. My "troublemaker frog" is now speaking and encouraging other youth ministries for the cause of reaching our world for Christ.

As I write this, I realize that most youth ministries have troublemakers like Ben, who attend and make our efforts challenging. The answer is not a quick-fix leadership position. The answer is found by investing in a person and standing by them as they grow through burned bridges and past mistakes. Investing yourself into someone should never be seen as a quick fix. Rather, it should be adopted as a way to help bring out the potential that is present in young people's lives.

JON PRITIKIN

Before

I first met Jon at a ski retreat while he was in high school. Jon was a tall, skinny young man who had trouble with the camp rules, especially the rules about staying out of the girls' cabins. It wasn't long before Jon and I had a run-in over his inability to conform to camp rules. I was direct in my description of the consequences should he be caught again. That night, Jon accepted Christ as Lord and Savior. I was privileged to be there with him as he prayed and accepted Christ as Lord and Savior.. Shortly after the camp ended I began discipleship with Jon. Jon also joined our power team and spent many hours a week with me in the gym and at my home talking about weightlifting and the things of God. Jon graduated high school and then went off to Bethany College to prepare for ministry.

After

Today, Jon is one of the Christian men that I look up to. He has grown in many ways. He is now 6′ 5″ and 310 pounds! He travels full time as an evangelist, breaking bricks and ice, as well as bending steel bars and tearing phone books. Jon is touching thousands of teens each year through his ministry. In addition, he also is involved with Donnie Moore, who is the team chaplain for the Oakland Athletics professional baseball team. Jon performs feats of strength with Donnie, and when the Athletics are playing a home game, he occasionally speaks to the players from both teams. He has a desire to win the lost that is almost unequaled. I occasionally am privileged with the opportunity to hear Jon speak at a public high school. Each time I watch him minister, tears come to my eyes, because Jon has built a ministry on believing in teens and investing himself into others' lives.

ABBY BLANKENSHIP

Before

When I first met Abby she had just left a youth group across town and started attending Crossfire. She was shy and made obvious attempts to stay clear of me. Over time, I learned that her last youth pastor had gone through a moral failure, and Abby was just one of the teens who had been left hurt and disillusioned. She was affected in many areas by this tragedy. Her confidence was almost nonexistent. Her trust level was also immeasurably low. It caused her to be emotional and cry over just about anything. But Abby was gifted in music. By allowing Abby to minister in this area, we were able to create a safe environment for her to experience habitual success. Little by little, she began to change. Before long she was a transformed young lady.

Over a period of months, Abby began to trust again. We finally were able to build a relationship. To this day, Abby still speaks with sorrow in her voice about her former youth group. Abby ended her high-school career leading a Christian club on one of our county's most violent and difficult campuses. In that position, she led many to Christ and provided a godly example that her school was desperate to see.

After

Today, Abby is serving her third year as an intern here at Crossfire. Her influence on young people is incredible. I have watched her grow to a level of great effectiveness in ministry. Abby now leads the youth choir, helps with the worship team, heads up all the campus ministries for eighteen schools, runs the discipleship program, and leads a Sunday school class. Abby is investing herself in the youth of our area.

These brief stories are significant to me. They continue to remind me of the value of investing myself into others. Every visitor I meet at Crossfire has the potential to become a Ben, Jon, or Abby. Youth pastor, it is vital that you invest yourself into the youth in your group!

3. You Will Succeed Only When Those around You Succeed

Too many leaders worry about making themselves look good. Tremendous amounts of energy are spent pushing themselves to the front, patting themselves on the backs, and making sure they are in the limelight. Those who possess this type of attitude will never succeed in equipping the saints. A leader must be interested in making others look good.

Invest yourself in others, and then allow them to succeed. Encourage, praise, and recognize others while you stand to the side. When this is your goal and motivation, those around you *will* succeed! As you invest in their lives, they begin to grow in their areas of responsibility. It is reciprocal: They grow, and they grow you. It's a win-win situation.

> **Too many leaders worry about making themselves look good.**

Winning situations in ministry only happen when we invest ourselves in others and then allow them the freedom to succeed and enjoy their success.

4. Don't Allow Other's Success to Threaten You

A huge deterrent to equipping and releasing people is pastoral insecurity. It is tragic to observe a pastor hoarding ministry responsibilities because he or she is afraid that somebody may outperform him or her. This petty insecurity must die if you are to fulfill Ephesians 4:11–16 in your ministry. My leadership team has been blessed with individuals who have incredible gifts and abilities, many of which I simply do not possess. They perform at a level of effectiveness that I cannot duplicate. Our approach in reaching the world with the gospel is well rounded. It is ridiculous to expect a pastor to excel in the pulpit in outreach, perform well at dramas, music, construction, visitation, cooking, small-group leadership, and drive the church bus. One individual cannot accomplish everything and maintain a cutting-edge, effective ministry. That is why we train the saints. As leaders, they will begin to influence other people. With influence comes love and loyalty to the person leading. All the youth in my ministry won't love and appreciate me, and I can't personally meet all their needs, but the only thing that matters is that those needs are met, even if they love and appreciate one of my leaders more than me.

> **I understand that all the youth in my ministry won't love and appreciate me.**

Crossfire's young teens sometimes think that my junior-high leader is the youth pastor. They love the junior-high director because of the time and investment he has made in their lives. That is the way it should be. Don't allow personal insecurities or the need to be the center of attention stop you from being obedient.

Ephesians 4:11–16 reveals a format to ensure blessing, effectiveness, and excitement in your youth ministry. Obedience in this area will prevent you from ineffectiveness and burnout.

chapter 4

I Can't Do This by Myself

Delegation vs. Ducking

Delegation brings incredible freedom to a leadership position. I have learned that the maximum number of people I can personally minister to each week is many times less than the actual number of young people who attend our weekly programs. The only way we can effectively meet the needs represented each week is to delegate responsibilities to other people. Delegation is a *skill* that must be learned, rather than an inborn quality in a leader. To develop the skill, you first must see the need and the advantages of it.

In my internship program, Master's Commission, I teach young people the significance of delegation in a very practical way. Each morning, I meet with my staff, give assignments for the day, and ask how their long-term projects are proceeding. I intentionally overload each intern's work schedule for a particular week. Without fail, each intern will approach me two or three days later and tell me it is impossible for them to accomplish all the tasks they were assigned. "I can't do this myself!" I simply agree with them, discuss the art of delegation,

Delegation will free you.

and help them assign different projects to different individuals, almost guaranteeing its completion. By doing this, an important thing happens: Their frustration and feelings of helplessness help them to learn the art of delegation. You will never delegate until you see the need.

Webster defines delegation as: "To send or remove from one place to another. A person authorized or sent to act for another" (*Webster's New Collegiate Dictionary,* 1977).

Delegation allows others to perform ministry and other assignments on your behalf. All too often I hear a well-meaning youth pastor say, "If I want it done right, I have to do it myself." Such a youth pastor is setting himself up for frustration, failure, and eventually burn-out. People think this self-reliant statement demonstrates a good work ethic or a concern about quality performance. However, the only thing that happens is that a lid is securely slapped on the potential of that ministry and those who sit under it. Friends, it is poor stewardship to not take advantage of all that has been entrusted to you.

Once I was asked to travel to a neighboring city to assist a small youth ministry with an evangelistic outreach. Dramas were rehearsed, a menu planned, a power team scheduled to come and break bricks, new convert packs created, and a follow-up plan put into place. Everything was set. Three days prior to the event the pastor of the church called and cancelled. I was shocked and more than just a little disappointed. I inquired as to why this had to happen. The pastor went on to explain that he had to be out of town that particular day and was unable to oversee the event. I tried to assure him that we would still come and do all we had prepared to do. I told him that I knew my leadership team and I could fill all the holes his absence would create. The pastor said, "Thank you, but I can't be there, and the way it works here is that unless I am here, nothing happens." The event was cancelled and was never rescheduled. I wish I could say this was an isolated instance, but the truth is, this is often the norm. Delegation will allow you to be in many places at one time, multiplying your efforts and effectiveness.

Delegation also means that other people are empowered and entrusted to make decisions. I am not the only guy who can make a decision. Currently 90 percent of the decisions in Crossfire are made before they get to me! People of different ages and leadership levels are capable of making decisions regarding their own areas, especially concerning activities, transportation, budgets, outreach locations, mission trip destinations, ministry purposes, leadership selection and training, and problem solving. By doing this, I am freed to do those things that only I am qualified to do.

Delegation is an awesome tool of leadership, but it shouldn't be confused with *ducking*. Ducking is simply dumping responsibilities on individuals and walking away. If this is your pattern, don't act surprised when staff members fail at their assignments. Ducking causes great confusion and eventual harm to your program.

Currently, 90 percent of the decisions in Crossfire are made before they get to me!

There is definitely a difference between delegation and ducking. Three things define delegation and make it work.

1. **Training**. It is inexcusable to release an individual into a task without first training that person. This is what I call setting a person up for success. Give them tools to succeed. If one of my staff members fails in a project, it is probably more my fault than theirs. People cannot do that which they do not know how to do.

2. **Release**. After an individual has been trained, they must be allowed to try their wings. Training without opportunity is pointless, like practicing every day after school with the baseball team but never being given the chance to play on Friday. Before long, one begins to lose interest and the desire fades. Make sure your leaders experience success.

   I have heard it said that failure is a great teacher. I disagree. Although I recognize one can learn from a mistake, nothing succeeds like success! Give tasks that build confidence, allow success, and prove that an individual's training and efforts are worthwhile. When one of your staff members succeeds, give him or her credit, praise, and recognition. Young people also need to learn how to handle success. Youth pastor, whatever you do, don't take credit for the work of another. Push them to the front and allow them to be in the spotlight. Release them to succeed. Then allow them to enjoy the fruits of their success.

3. **Follow Up**. This important step makes all the difference between success and failure. Each time you assign a task to an individual, it is vitally

important to have an evaluation time afterward. Discuss things that went well and areas that could stand improvement next time. Never use the phrase "What you did wrong." Your staff person or teen must know that you care and actually believe in helping them achieve success. More learning takes place in the follow-up stage than in the previous two combined. People are concerned about the quality of their performance. Help your staff to see the big picture and understand how you view the overall needs of the ministry. Fol-low-up is often neglected, but it is significant for helping your people learn and prepare themselves for future assignments.

> **Although I recognize one can learn from a mistake, nothing succeeds like success!**

At Crossfire, we currently have eighty separate ministries that operate under the umbrella of youth ministry. The leadership of each of these ministries has been delegated to a young person. Without delegation, none of this would be possible. It is great to watch others reach their potential as together you impact your community for Christ.

chapter 5

Reproducing
What Are You Reproducing?

Flesh gives birth to flesh, but spirit gives birth to spirit. (John 3:6)

Many aspects of a successful youth ministry are so simple, so logical, that we simply choose to ignore them. Instead, we search for more romantic ways of producing success in our eyes. I know youth pastors who constantly search for the perfect drama, just the right song or anointed sermon notes to transform their youth ministry. But more important than the latest song or drama is the *spirit* of the youth leader.

John 3:6 teaches that flesh gives birth to flesh and spirit gives birth to spirit. As I visit with youth ministers and their wives, I have noticed it is common for them to have children. Just as they give birth to children, in the same way, their spirit reproduces in those under their influence. Before long, your group will demonstrate attitudes and character traits much like your own. Do you possess attitudes and character qualities you want

51

to see in the lives of your students and leadership? Before we worry about great attendance, concern ourselves with image, or powerful speaking or touching kids for Christ, we need to concern ourselves with our own character and integrity. Reputation is what others say about you, but character is who you really are. You cannot build a youth program on your reputation. You must have character.

> **Do you possess attitudes and character qualities you want to see in the lives of your students and leadership?**

Character is determined by how you act when nobody is looking. How do you handle the little responsibilities in life? For example, your private devotions are the most public thing you will ever do. Little things mean a lot. The ordinary, when touched by God, becomes extraordinary. Attention to these seemingly insignificant areas will determine the difference between effectiveness and failure. Significance in the ordinary? Ask Goliath about the significance of a single stone. Or ask Peter about the common event of a rooster crowing. How about bread and fish in the hands of Jesus? Or three commonplace spikes used by Roman soldiers. Ordinary every one of them. But add God's touch and they become significant, relevant, and life changing. So it is with your devotions, your character, and your integrity: They are simple, ordinary, and steeped in significance.

Spirit gives birth to spirit. Often, one's spirit can be discerned simply by observing one's youth ministry. It doesn't matter how much charisma you have in front of others or how well you speak. You may make students laugh and cry at the same time. Your services might compel them to the altars every week. But who are you when nobody is watching? Spirit gives birth to spirit. Kind of a scary thought, isn't it? They will become whatever you are, not what you wish you were or what you hope to become. No matter how you camouflage it, your spirit will be produced in your congregation.

Several years ago, I went through an extremely difficult time in my ministry. I was working very hard, and we were just starting to see some signs of change and positive growth. During this time, one of my interns became angry and unhappy over an issue that I don't understand to this day. Within a matter of weeks, he caused a division throughout my entire youth ministry. My thought life regarding this person was less than pure. When I turned to Scripture for comfort, I found the verses regarding how to treat an enemy. I chose to forgive and pray for blessings in his life. I chose not to insult him in private or in public. I was doing all the right things on the outside, but inside I was wounded. In the middle of this conflict was the Northern California/Nevada District Council for the Assemblies of God. I seriously debated whether or not to attend because of the turmoil my ministry was experiencing. At the last minute, I decided to make the trip, all the while hoping that God would fix the problem.

In my hotel room that night I began to cry. Nothing spiritual about it, it was just self-pity. At that time God spoke to me and

Reputation is what others say about you, but character is who you really are.

said, *Do you want a ministry filled with people drowning in self-pity? Do you want a ministry of fear? Do you want a ministry that focuses only on hurts and disappointments? Do*

53

you want your ministry filled with resentment, anger, and bitterness? Do you want to lead a ministry that limits itself because of what might happen? That was the night I realized my spirit is not just my business; my spirit affects those around me. I changed my attitude that night, not just for me, but also for the youth I love and to whom I minister. Whatever you are, that's who they will become. Period.

- If you are a person of prayer, they will be too
- If you love evangelism, so will they
- If you love the lost, so will they
- If you see visitors as VIPs, they will to
- If you love God's Word, so will they
- If you are honest and vulnerable, they will be

But

- If you are critical, they will be too
- If you try to slide by, so will they
- If you look for shortcuts, so will they
- If you lead with manipulation, they will live that way
- If you are dishonest, they will be too

The Bible tells us in direct fashion, "Not many of you should presume to be teachers, my brothers, because you know that we who teach will be judged more strictly" (James 3:1).

A young lady came to our youth group about a year ago. To say she had problems would be a total understatement. She was part of a vampire cult in our area and had been abused physically, spiritually, and emotionally. It took months to win her trust and lead her to Christ.

One year ago, a certain young man participated in drive-by shootings to prove loyalty to his gang. He came in hard and hurt, trusting nobody. He doubted the purest of intentions. After a year, he was in love with Jesus and doing great.

In these two brief bios, you have met two students in my ministry. Don't they have enough of a past to overcome? Don't they have enough issues without me birthing negativity into them? Spirit gives birth to spirit. What are you birthing into your kids?

chapter 6

Faithful and Able

You then, my son, be strong in the grace that is in Christ Jesus. And the things you have heard me say in the presence of many witnesses entrust to reliable men who will also be qualified to teach others. (2 Timothy 2:1–2)

These scriptures outline a simple principle in selecting leaders. This principle applies to all levels of leadership. Early in my ministry, I selected some wrong people for leadership positions. I then became frustrated with young people who experienced moral failures in drugs, sex, alcohol, and rebellion while on the leadership team in my youth ministry. I talked with them, held them accountable, placed them on probation, assigned devotions, and sent them to professional counselors. I was content in my struggle. I thought I was doing everything right when, all of a sudden, my world was rocked by the moral failure of one of my most promising leaders.

I loved and invested very heavily in this individual. His pornography addiction led to stealing and breaking into houses. Eventually, his lust drove him to prostitutes in the downtown area. When the news reached me, I cried for days. Devastation hit this young man's life, and the effects of it ran through my youth ministry. I knew that there had to be a better way to qualify leadership before investing heavily in their lives.

All too often, we get caught up on a person's ability.

Then I discovered the truth of 2 Timothy 2:1–2. One principle is repeated over and over again in Scripture: A person must be faithful and able. This applies to leadership of all ages and all levels: junior-high leadership, senior-high leadership, youth interns, adult youth workers, junior-high pastors, and youth pastors. All too often, we get caught up on a person's *ability*. We notice things like their ability to sing well or their talent in drama. Perhaps they have a class B driver's license to drive the church bus, are a good communicator, relate well with the teens, or have a lot of money to help with our program. It is easy to focus on the things that people can give, but according to this scripture, that is the secondary concern.

Our primary concern is, how faithful they have been to God with the gifts they have been entrusted. Our focus has to change from what they can give to me, to what have they given to Thee? People who have ability but lack faithfulness will prove to be a curse in any ministry.

Let's examine these two words to gain a better understanding of their significance.

- *Faithful.* Worthy of trust, honest, loyal. Reliable, accurate, dependable, exact, true.
- *Able.* Capable of being, worthy of being, tending or inclined to.

Faithfulness then becomes a prerequisite to ability.

Now it is required that those who have been given a trust must prove faithful. (1 Corinthians 4:2)

Whoever can be trusted with very little can also be trusted with much, and whoever is dishonest with very little will also be dishonest with much. So if you have not been trustworthy in handling worldly wealth, who will trust you with true riches? And if you have not been trustworthy with someone else's property, who will give you property of your own? (Luke 16:10–12)

Stop judging by mere appearances, and make the right judgment. (John 7:24)

Faithfulness is the acid test for leadership.

History unfolds in 1 Samuel 16 when the prophet Samuel comes to Bethlehem to anoint a new king. Needless to say, his presence caused quite a stir. In just a few short hours, a sacrifice was prepared and Jesse and his sons prepared themselves according to Jewish tradition to attend the ceremony. As Jesse had his son Eliab pass in front of the prophet, God spoke to

> **Our focus has to change from what they can give me, to what have they given to Thee.**

Samuel, "Do not consider his appearance or his height, for I have rejected him. The Lord does not look at the things man looks at. Man looks at the outward appearances, but God looks at the heart" (1 Samuel 16:7). Seven of Jesse's sons passed in front of Samuel and, one by one, all were rejected by God.

But later, David was sent for. He arrived dirty, sweating, and out of breath. His outward appearance was incorrect for the occasion. But in verse 12, God said, "Arise and anoint him; he is the one." Why? Faithfulness! David could have been sitting on the Judean hills with sheep and a bad attitude about his job. He could have been smoking pot as he watched the sheep. But he didn't do any of those things. He was faithful in his duties. He used that time to refine skills that God would use. He played a harp, sang praises, took care of shepherding responsibilities, practiced with his sling, and became a man after God's own heart. He was faithful in little things, ordinary things, resulting in promotion to a palace.

Faithfulness yields effectiveness in ministry. For this reason, I have developed the following questionnaire to help me determine the faithfulness of potential youth leadership. These ten simple questions have saved me much pain and regret. I encourage you to utilize a standard tool like this to help you determine if potential workers are faithful and able.

Faithfulness Test
Youth Worker

1. How do you handle family responsibility? (Including spouse, parents, and siblings)
2. Do you tithe? Are you financially faithful?
3. How long have you had your present job? What is the longest you have been employed at one place?

4. Do you help with other ministries? How did you do? Are you a good helper, or are you just interested in being in charge?
5. Will you provide a letter of recommendation from your former pastor regarding your former ministry experience?
6. Do you share your faith? When was the last time you led somebody to Christ?
7. Do you attend church consistently?
8. How regular are you with devotions? How regular with prayer?
9. Do you honor God and His principles in your relationships with the opposite sex?
10. Are you willing to be fingerprinted and to fill out a background questionnaire as required by California State law?

chapter 7

Urgent vs. Important

When I first began in youth ministry, my father pulled me aside and issued this warning to me, "Your greatest danger in ministry is letting the urgent tasks crowd out those that are really important." I walked away that day with a huge question mark in my mind and no reference to help me understand his pearl of wisdom. In the past several years of full-time youth ministry, those words have often returned to haunt and rebuke me as I tried to determine what was urgent and what was truly important.

As ministers, we live in constant tension because we have a limited number of hours each day. As demands are made on our lives, we have to understand that some important tasks don't need to be done today. Some tasks can wait until next week or next month, but urgent demands always seem to call for an immediate response. Without fail, the urgent will destroy your time, energy, and resources—the tyranny of urgency. This battle was present in the life of one of the most effective leaders of

the Old Testament: Moses. In Exodus 18:13–24 we read
that Moses had huge demands placed upon him as he
governed Israel. Moses' important task was to guide the
people to be what God wanted them to become, but the
urgent pressed in. Look at what was taking all of Moses'
time:

- v 13. Moses served as the only judge over almost
  three million people and alone judged the people
  from morning to evening
- v 16. He handled disputes between the people
  and informed the people of God's laws and
  decrees

I love Jethro, Moses' father-in-law, because he understood the dilemma. Moses had become distracted by the
demands. Although he was doing good things, he was
not the only one who
could take care of all
the leadership tasks.
Jethro introduced a
plan to divide the load
and involve other men
as judges, allowing
Moses to accomplish
the things God had
called him to do.

**Without fail, the
urgent will destroy
your time, energy,
and resources—the
tyranny of urgency.**

Moses learned that *delegation* enabled him to focus on
the things that he did best.

From this snapshot into Moses' life, we are reminded
that we all have limited amounts of money, time, and
energy. We are to be wise stewards to gain the most effective results possible with what we have been given.

Many times in the New Testament, Jesus announced
that He did not come to carry out His own plans, but
rather, to carry out the plans of God.

For I have come down from heaven not to do my will but to do the will of Him who sent me. (John 6:38)

. . . I do nothing on my own but speak just what the Father has taught me. The One who has sent me is with me; He has not left me alone, for I always do what pleases Him. (John 8:28–29)

How did Jesus go about setting priorities that would govern His ministry and make these incredible claims actually come to pass? We find the answer in Mark 1:21–39.

They went to Capernaum, and when the Sabbath came, Jesus went into the synagogue and began to teach. The people were amazed at his teaching, because he taught them as one who had authority, not as the teachers of the law. Just then a man in their synagogue who was possessed by an evil spirit cried out, "What do you want with us, Jesus of Nazareth? Have you come here to destroy us? I know who you are—the Holy One of God!"

"Be quiet!" said Jesus sternly. "Come out of him!" The evil spirit shook the man violently and came out of him with a shriek.

The people were all so amazed that they asked each other, "What is this? A new teaching—and with authority! He even gives orders to the evil spirits and they obey him." News about him spread quickly over the whole region of Galilee. As soon as they left the synagogue, they went with James and John to the home of Simon and Andrew. Simon's mother-in-law was in bed with a fever, and they told Jesus about her. So he went to her, took her hand and helped her up. The fever left her and she began to wait on them. That evening after sunset the people brought to Jesus all the sick and demon-possessed. The whole town gathered at the door, and Jesus healed many who had various diseases. He also drove out many demons, but he would not let them speak because they knew who he was.

Very early in the morning, while it was till dark, Jesus got up, left the house and went off to a solitary place, where he prayed. Simon and his companions went to look for him, and when they found him, they exclaimed: "Everyone is looking for you!"

Jesus replied, "Let us go somewhere else—to the nearby villages—so I can preach there also. That is why I have come." So he traveled throughout Galilee, preaching in their synagogues and driving out demons.

This passage shows Jesus doing what He does best: changing lives. Jesus is preaching and casting out demons, then visits Simon's home and heals his mother-in-law. After the activity of the day, the sick and demon-possessed visited to be healed. Jesus helped them too. What a day! Ever had one of those days when the demands just won't stop? People need more than you have to give, yet they want more. Welcome to the tyranny of the urgent. If you have ever felt less than Superman, just wanted peace and quiet in your ministry, then you will appreciate Mark 1:35.

Very early in the morning, while it was still dark, Jesus got up, left the house and went to a solitary place, where he prayed.

Jesus knew what was important and what was urgent because He kept God as His number one priority. Jesus was desperate to be alone with God! Our society loves noise: radios, television, CD players, and telephones—on and on it goes. How tragic that we seldom experience silence. Psalm 46:10 assures us that when we are still, we will know God. Jesus was alone with God, doing what was important. About this time, Simon burst on the scene. "Everyone is looking for you!" Would you like the modern translation? "Jesus where have you been? What do you think you are doing out here? There are more needs you must meet."

The answer Jesus gave shocked the disciples. It still shocks many today who read this passage. "Let's go somewhere else—to nearby villages—so I can preach there also.

> **Time alone with God allowed Christ to defeat the tyranny of the urgent in His life.**

That is why I have come." The time that Jesus had experienced alone with God allowed him to decide what was important. It was a time of refreshing and refocusing on why he had come. As they left to do what was important, they walked away from a demanding crowd with urgent needs. Time alone with God allowed Christ to defeat the tyranny of the urgent in His life.

I don't know about you, but I battle over this issue of the important versus the urgent. I hate to say no to people. I don't like turning my back on needy situations. But there are times we may have to do that to stay focused on what is truly important. As ministers we must understand:

- Needs *don't* dictate our ministries.
- Demands *don't* dictate our ministries.
- Opinions *don't* dictate our ministries.
- Tragedies and disasters *don't* dictate our ministries.
- *Only* the call of God and what he labels as important dictates our ministries.

My friend Benny Perez once told me, "God's opinion makes man's opinion irrelevant. Find out what God is saying about you." God will never call you to the urgent. His call will always be based on that which is most important.

Recently, I received a phone call at my home at 2:00 A.M. I answered the phone and awoke to a fast-paced, high-pitched voice that was explaining a family problem she was experiencing. "Pastor, you must come over here right now! We need you to pray." I calmly asked how long that this family problem had been an issue. I was told that it had been this way for several months. I agreed to pray about this need over the phone, but refused to leave my home. I prayed and set a 10:00 A.M. appointment for the next morning so that I could help with this tragedy. I then hung up and went back to sleep. The next day, 10:00 A.M. came and went. My appointment never showed. I called their home and inquired about what had happened to cause them to miss our meeting. "Oh pastor—we decided not to come in. Everything worked itself out last night after we got off the phone." The urgent will take all you have to give and then demand more. There are matters that are important. You can't do both. Follow the examples of Moses and Jesus: Do the important!

chapter 8

Junior-High Leadership

They Can if You will Let Them

At first, this seems to be an oxymoron. The images that come to mind when one says "junior higher" cover a wide range, producing reluctance, even fear, in the minds of many. Seldom do people equate words like *responsible*, *mature*, *leadership*, *aware*, *caring*, *capable*, and *dependable* with the junior-high members of a youth ministry. That mindset needs to change.

I have learned to love and appreciate the junior-high segment of my youth ministry. I have also learned that within junior-high students is a vast hidden treasure of potential and possibility just waiting to be released. I have encountered many youth ministries that do next to nothing with the junior-high segment of their program. They are just waiting for them to age two more years so they can become "real" youth group members. If that is your mindset, you probably need a career change. You should invest in and help release the potential of all the youth under your care. In 1 Timothy 4:12 we are instructed very clearly not to look down on youth. Please don't dismiss a young person because they are awkward and trying to catch up with their latest growth spurt.

Rather, find their value and help them learn to minister. I have learned a valuable lesson in this area. I have personally witnessed the fact that junior-high students can become productive members of the youth ministry by seventh grade, instead of waiting until the middle of their senior-high school career.

Seldom, if ever, do people equate words like *responsible, mature, leadership, aware, caring, capable*, and *dependable* with the junior-high members of a youth ministry.

Junior-high leadership teams will enrich your entire youth ministry. As junior-high youth perform, they do an interesting thing to the rest of your leadership teams. It puts pressure on them to perform at a higher level so that they are not outdone by the young teens. This level of leadership is an excellent training ground for young people to learn leadership skills and to experience the joy and success of leadership.

Before we get into the specifics of how to lead a junior-high leadership team, I want to introduce you to some of the junior-high leaders at Crossfire.

JEFF PRYOR, AGE 13, HILLVIEW MIDDLE SCHOOL

Jeff Pryor lives a life of consistency that is rivaled by few. It doesn't matter what it is or when it is, if Jeff says something, he will do it. It is difficult to depend on people today. Many people have busy schedules. Jeff also has a busy life, but he is always honest and true to what he says. His personality is contagious, and he is kind and pleasant to be around. He is simply the kind of young person that is a joy to be with. There is nothing Jeff cannot do, because he sincerely puts his trust and hope in the strength of God.

Jeff leads the junior-high prayer request ministry.

MADISON ALTAMIRANO, AGE 13, DIABLO VIEW MIDDLE SCHOOL

One of the most shining, exciting young people you will ever meet is Madison Altamirano. As a seventh grader, she models to other junior-high students what it means to have the joy of the Lord as your strength. Each day, Madison grows closer and closer to Christ. She has a sincere desire to have a strong relationship with Him. There is truly no limit to the things she can accomplish with the abilities and potential God has placed in her life. She is a wonderful example of a Christian who is sincerely excited to serve the Lord.

Madison leads the junior-high phone call follow-up ministry for girls.

ANNA JACKSON, AGE 13, YGNACIO VALLEY CHRISTIAN SCHOOL

Anna is a beautiful model of faithfulness in a world of uncaring, unfaithful people. Her desire to serve God and know Him intimately is obvious as she ministers to others in every part of her life. Whether at school, church, or home, she walks her talk. Anna is not simply a casual Christian who is apathetic and bored with her faith. She actively shares Christ with those who are lost. She faithfully devotes time to God. She tirelessly encourages and builds up those around her. Her life radiates the love of God as she strives daily to become closer to Him.

Anna leads the junior-high birthday and flyer ministries.

CURTIS RUIZ, AGE 13, YGNACIO VALLEY CHRISTIAN SCHOOL

There are very few young people who have the potential that Curtis does. He is an extremely well rounded young man who desires to grow closer to God each day. He has a willing spirit that is consistent and easy to work with. He is bold in sharing his faith with anyone who will listen. He does not stop at the status quo, but pursues excellence in everything he does. Curtis is looked up to and admired by literally hundreds of teens because of the incredibly consistent life he lives. His love for others shows, and he is faithful to act on the opportunities God gives him.

Curtis leads the junior-high phone call follow-up ministry for boys.

◊◊◊

I love these people. They are an incredible testimony to what young people can be to their school, families, and their youth group.

The following items are essential in the development of a junior-high leadership team.

1. Speak Value into Their Lives

This is key. At this difficult time in life it is important to let junior-high students know that they have significance. There are few things that will make a bigger difference in one of these students' lives than to speak value into them. Make it a goal in the leadership events and activities that they lead to speak value into each of the young leaders' lives.

2. Make Them Feel Special

To a junior-high student love is spelled T-I-M-E.

T—TRUTHFUL

Be truthful in everything you tell them, even when it hurts. As a girl on my junior-high team once said, "You tell me what I need to hear, not just what I want to hear."

Youth appreciate our honesty. They want to focus everything on Jesus, because He said, "I am the way, the truth, and the life" (John 14:6). Jesus is in favor of the truth and is the inventor of truth because He is the truth! "Then you will know the truth and the truth will set you free" (John 8:32). Be truthful. Your kids are dying to see truth in action.

I—INVEST

Our goal must be to deposit part of our own lives into the lives of young people. This can only be accomplished by giving freely of one's self—your valuable resources, such as time, money, and attention. This means making yourself vulnerable and open to rejection. Every great investment opportunity requires an element of risk. I love to watch the results of great investments. Teenagers who know they are loved and experience the true love of Jesus become incredible tools of the Lord. They are so alive, energetic, unafraid, extreme, and totally real! What more could you want in an army to help spread the good news of Jesus Christ?

M—MENTOR

"Follow my example, as I follow the example of Christ" (1 Corinthians 11:1). Our goal has to be to set an example that others can follow. By doing so, our youth will see Jesus in our example. Mentorship extends beyond Sunday mornings and Wednesday nights. It means allowing your home, your marriage, your family, your opinions, and the way you handle problems to be studied and imitated. It's making kids feel important by spending more one-on-one time, the precious commodity that few are willing to give to them. People don't care how much you know until they know how much you care.

E—ENCOURAGE

Do you remember how it was, all the difficulties of home, school, relationships, and a constantly changing body? It's hard for me to remember until I come face to face with it in almost every teenager that I meet. Encouragement is a valuable tool that can help people through more situations than anything else. This tool was used many times by Jesus, by Paul, by God, and many others throughout Scripture. Encouragement does things for individuals that nothing else will ever do. In the world, encouragement is as rare as a flawless diamond on the streets. Our society tears down self-image, self-worth, and self-esteem. But you have the weapon of encouragement to combat and reverse the effects of this godless society.

3. Make Sure They Succeed

Create an environment of habitual success. Nothing succeeds like success. Make sure that your young leaders experience it often. This is totally under your control. As you set your goals and make your assignments for the leadership team, keep in mind that you are setting them up to succeed.

4. Show Them Leadership Is Fun

Too many things in life have no zest, no zip, and no fun. Leadership is exciting. Junior-high students are interested in having a good time at whatever they do. Your leadership meetings, assignments, and ministry responsibilities must be seasoned with a lot of good times. If junior-high students are not laughing occasionally, it's simply too heavy for them. Keep it fun!

5. Whet Their Appetite for Future Ministry

This is an introductory level to leadership. You are preparing young lives for future leadership opportunities. Our goal at this age is to capture their attention and imagination. They need to be excited by the opportunities that you afford them, and they always should be left wanting more.

> **Encouragement is a valuable tool that can help people through more situations than anything else.**

6. Keep Them from Heavy Responsibility

Our goal isn't to burn them out. Don't overload them with unnecessary work and responsibility. No assignments should be given that would ever discourage or dishearten the leadership potential of a junior-high student.

7. Set Definite Standards of Accountability

In a day of loose standards, nonexistent morals, and no boundaries, it's important that we set expectations and accountability. Insist upon a level of excellence in everything these young teens do. When excellence is not obtained they need to learn and understand that standards demand it be done correctly. At the end of this chapter, you will find a copy of our junior-high leadership requirements and a copy of the junior-high handbook that all of our junior-high leaders are required to carry.

8. Stress Group Leadership over Individual Accomplishment

This level of leadership isn't intended to create heroes, but rather, to create a winning team and winning atmosphere. This means that you allow the group to succeed *together*, depending upon each other to accomplish tasks and experience victories and failures. No junior-high student can handle being singled out as a hero. It will go to his head, and he will eventually experience failure. As a team, they will strengthen each other through success.

9. Show Them How to Lead by Following Your Leader

Your future followers in your leadership will follow the way you followed those in authority over you. This is a vital truth that must be taught at an early age. Teach them the value of following well. It will determine how others follow them. Submitting to authority is a learned thing, and we must teach it to our leaders. Follow well so you can lead well.

10. Give Opportunity to Learn from Mistakes

We have all heard that mistakes are the only thing you can truly call your own. In addition, the only thing that brings value to mistakes is your ability to learn from them. It is up to the youth pastor to turn mistakes into learning opportunities. When a mistake occurs, don't overreact. Discuss the problem and how it could have been handled differently. You have earned the right to speak into their lives; don't miss the opportunity.

Junior-High Youth Council (Firestarters)
Leadership Requirements

- Attend monthly dinner, including a devotion and youth/junior-high business discussion.
- Faithfully attend youth functions, services, and Sunday school.
- Have a ministry within the junior-high department. Ministries are overseen by the junior-high director.

- Demonstrate a consistently good attitude and support the leadership. Set a good example for other junior-high students to follow.

Firestarter's Contract

Firestarters is a group of junior-high students who are committed to supporting Crossfire Youth Ministries and the Junior High Department of Crossfire. In view of 1 Timothy 4:12, they set an example for other junior-high students in the areas of speech, life, love, faith, and purity. They are also faithful in attendance and support of Crossfire and junior high. They have a strong walk with God and are committed to sharing the message with friends.

chapter 9

Senior-High Leadership

The Backbone of Your Youth Ministry

This is my favorite topic in youth ministry. Senior-high leadership will provide the backbone of your ministry. They possesses all the ability, excitement, energy, and motivation needed to lead ministries, services, campus clubs, worship teams, visitation teams, and discipleship for the new converts. This level of your leadership team will, in fact, determine the success or failure of your own leadership. Successful youth ministry means allowing your youth to take ownership of the youth program. The more they own it, the more excited they become about what's going on. The more excited they are, the more they will invite their unsaved friends. The effort and energy that is spent in developing this level of leadership is guaranteed to pay rich dividends.

The youth pastor who insists on being the center of attention, the main man, the entertainer, and the only one up front, simply makes me shudder. This is the type of youth pastor who is afraid to release the control of anything to his youth. It makes me sad when I visit a youth ministry and I see the youth pastor with the microphone in his hand from the first minute until the last minute of his service. Why would teens run to see that kind of a service? They sit in classrooms like that six times a day. When the bell rings they can't wait to escape. Your youth ministry must be different than what they see every day at school.

If the program is boring, your students won't humiliate themselves by bringing their friends to a dead zone.

Here's an idea: Let the senior-high students be involved in the service. When they are involved they are excited. When they tell their friends, they come. When their friends come, your group begins to grow. This isn't rocket science. Kids won't come to something they don't like. If the program is boring, your students won't humiliate themselves by bringing their friends to a dead zone. The best way to put electricity in the air is to give real responsibility to the youth in your care. Then, and only then, will they own it. And when they own it, it gets exciting.

Let me introduce you to four of my senior-high leaders. Here is what they have to say about this style of youth ministry.

ANDREA AINSWORTH, AGE 18, CLAYTON VALLEY HIGH SCHOOL

Being a Pacesetter has been an incredible learning experience for me. It has helped me to grow in so many ways.

In my junior year, when I became a Pacesetter, I was given the opportunity to head the altar-worker's ministry. This is a big responsibility, and I was a little intimidated.

But through prayer, tons of questions, and lots of hard work, my life, as well as hundreds of other lives, has been radically altered through this ministry.

Being in charge of altar workers has taught me responsibility, organization, effective prayer, and one-on-one discipleship. All these lessons have helped me grow stronger in Christ and will be invaluable later on.

As a Pacesetter I have learned to be a leader. For a long time I wasn't a person that would take the initiative. I was scared of what others would think of me and how they would treat me. Being a Pacesetter has shown me how to stand up for what I believe in. God has taken the fear away and has given me the awesome gift of leadership.

There has been a noticeable change in my walk with God since I have been a Pacesetter. Daily, I want to spend more time with Him. Knowing that, as a leader, others are watching me has made me realize that I need to walk with Christ daily so others can see Christ in me.

These are only a few examples of how being a Pacesetter has been a great learning experience. Mentally and spiritually my life has changed for the better. God has truly blessed me with the opportunity of being in this leadership position.

DAVID GRAHAM, AGE 15, CLAYTON VALLEY HIGH SCHOOL

Though I have been a Pacesetter for only a short while, it has greatly impacted me. From the very start, my fellow leaders have been there for me. They've driven me to practices, asked me how I was feeling when I didn't look so good, encouraged me, and shown me love whenever I was near them. In many ways I depended on them, and in many ways they depended on me. I've also very much enjoyed the dinners at Pastor Bret's house, with great food and great fellowship with him, the other Pacesetters, and Matt and Brian.

Being in leadership has given me more responsibility. It has put me in a position where I have people that depend on me. This has caused me to grow and become more responsible.

Being a Pacesetter has forced me to adopt a much higher standard for my life. Leadership has taught me to have daily devotions, which has significantly helped my relationship with God and with other people. Because of leadership, I'm more faithful in my attendance to services and activities, and I'm more faithful with my duties at the church as well. Leadership has allowed me to go on many outreaches and activities where I've been able to bring people to Christ and grow in my relationship with God and my fellow workers in Christ.

Being a Pacesetter has been a great experience, and I look forward to what this year will hold.

CHRISTY PRYOR, AGE 17, CARONDELET HIGH SCHOOL

For the past two years I have had the privilege of serving on Pacesetters, Crossfire's high-school leadership group. As a Pacesetter, I am very involved in Crossfire and have many responsibilities in the youth group. I also have become a stronger Christian and have grown tremendously in my walk with Christ as a result. I am honored to be able to work in such a great youth ministry and am thankful for all the opportunities that I have been given to lead and excel in my leadership abilities, as well as grow spiritually.

Being a Pacesetter is a very important part of my life, partly due to the fact that I spend a considerable amount of my time on activities and ministries for Pacesetters and Crossfire. However, being on Pacesetters is more than just doing things around the church and going on youth trips and outreaches because it is expected of me. For me, Pacesetters is being used by God to help serve and minister with Crossfire in any way He wants me to, being willing to learn about Christian leadership and servanthood at the same time. Christ was a leader, and He led by serving. In Pacesetters, I have learned about the importance of servanthood and humility in leadership. I've been given opportunities to serve with humility in the ministries I lead. Even simply around Crossfire, I am there to serve, helping out wherever I can. Having Christ as my example, I'm learning how to become a better servant.

One part of Pacesetters that I really enjoy is our monthly Pacesetter dinner. Though they are fun times of fellowship and eating at Pastor Bret's house, they are also times of learning and training. At every dinner, we have a devotion time and we study and discuss topics and areas that pertain to our leadership and training. Recently, we have been focusing on the successes and failures of leaders in the Bible and what we can learn from them. I have enjoyed learning the qualities of a good leader and am glad I have been made aware of some of the pitfalls and areas where Satan tries to attack leaders, so I can be on my guard. Personally, I have been able to examine my own life and work on areas that need improvement for me to become the leader Christ wants me to be, as well as get rid of things in my life that would hinder and hurt my leadership.

Successful youth ministry means allowing your youth to take ownership of the youth program.

Working at the altars and praying with people to accept Christ into their lives is another part of being a Pacesetter that I like a lot. It is exciting for me each time I get to sit down with a girl to pray and talk with her about Christ. Seeing people

83

make a commitment to Christ for the first time, as well as rededicating their life to Christ, is an awesome experience and is something I enjoy greatly. The look on their faces when we say amen is unforgettable. It's fun to talk with them and share my own personal testimony of how Christ has transformed my life.

Every week I have to turn devotion sheets into Pastor Bret, one for each day's devotions for the entire week. It has become something that I really enjoy, because it not only helps not to skip a day's devotions, but it also causes me to really think about and take in what I'm reading. Writing about the verse that was the most meaningful for me on a particular day and how it relates to me personally is something that I look forward to every day. I like writing about a verse, and in some cases, a few verses, because it causes me to think closely about the verse and how it applies to my own life. Many times throughout a week, I find verses that stick out to me. When I think and write about them, I discover that they relate to other verses I have read earlier in the week and deal with some of the issues that God has been speaking to me about. Patience and waiting upon the Lord, praising and worshiping God, and not being afraid are just a few of the topics I've noticed some of my verses to be about.

I think another reason why I like doing the devotion sheets so much is that when I turn them into Pastor Bret, he reads them and writes comments back. I get encouragement from his comments, as well as words of wisdom. Sometimes he writes personal little notes. Sometimes he adds other scripture references that talk about a similar subject. And sometimes he gives encouraging little sayings that deal with what I wrote about. The devotion sheets definitely aid my spiritual growth, and I like them a lot.

Pacesetters are very special to me, and I'm glad I have had the opportunity to serve and minister in Crossfire.

Knowing that people believe in me means a lot to me. I like that I've been given leadership training as well as ministries to lead to put what I learned into practice. The learning and growing that I have experienced has been immense, and I am so happy to be able to serve on leadership as a Pacesetter.

MEAGAN HENSLEY, AGE 17, NORTHGATE HIGH SCHOOL

The Pacesetters program represents a standard of leadership that is being raised in a world of inadequately equipped high-school-aged ministers. Pacesetters stop following the trends and start setting the pace. The Pacesetters program provides leadership training that is not available to most high-school students. Pacesetters have the opportunity to lead their own ministry and be a large part of what goes on in the youth group. Pacesetters make important decisions that decide where the youth group will go for the summer mission trips. Pacesetters will mold and shape the student that is willing to sacrifice his or her time and energy in service to God.

In my own life, Pacesetters has made me who I am today. Raising a standard of excellence has become high priority for me. Being a Pacesetter, I have also learned a lot about servanthood, humility, and my availability to Christ.

I was so surprised when I was chosen for Pacesetters, because I had only been a Christian for a short while. When I began Pacesetters, I had no idea how to lead or where to begin. I was always the one that took from people, instead of giving to people. In this program, my relationship with God has grown beyond my expectations. In the ministries that I am involved with through Pacesetters, I have grown in servanthood. My time with God has become intimate, and God has helped me to have an honest humility with Him, where He can mold me and change me according to His will for my life. The daily devotion sheets that we have to fill out and turn in have kept me in line and on track when I could have easily lost focus. Because of all the great lessons that I have been taught through our Pacesetter devotions once a month, I have been able to gain insight on how to better lead my campus club at Northgate High School and lead the phone ministry for Crossfire. I have developed close friendships with other Pacesetters who have helped me to be accountable. As a body, we have developed a unity and a sense of family. Being a Pacesetter has been an awesome opportunity to be on a leadership team that raises the standard and sets the pace for a lost and dying world.

◊◊◊

I firmly believe in this philosophy. Below is a list of responsibilities that have been, or currently are, led by senior-high students.

- Worship team leader
- Worship team/band member
- Altar workers
- Announcements
- Welcome visitors ("Welcome Wagon")
- Greeters
- Special music
- Offering
- Campus clubs
- Small group leaders
- Information booth
- Visitation team
- Human videos
- Illustrated sermons

- Dance ministry
- Lighting
- Sound
- Phone ministry
- Street dramas
- Prayer ministries

Senior-high students have the same needs that junior-high students have who are in leadership. They need boundaries and expectations set for them. The following is the standard that my senior-high leadership is expected to follow.

My Expectations
The Standard for Crossfire Pacesetters

- Involved in drama or music ministry
- Lead a ministry
- Attend Crossfire, Riot, and Sunday P.M. services (consistently)
- Attend outreaches
- Attend activities
- Participate in altar calls
- Help in greeting line
- Devotions from Pacesetter book
- Read chapter for meeting each month. Bring notes on the reading
- 3.0 GPA
- No unexcused absences from activities. Call me. Talk to me. Let me know. Two unexcused = probation for one month. Missing during probation = done
- Drugs, alcohol, sex = done. No probation
- Each Thursday, hand in devotion sheets. Fill in info honestly. Leaders are accountable to others.

I want you to be accountable for this area of your life

- Pre-service prayer @ 6:30 P.M.
- Support pastors and Master's Commission in action, attitude, and participation
- Be on time to activities—for Pacesetters that means 30 minutes early. Being late shows a lack of respect and makes a statement on the importance of what we are doing.
- Carry and use your Pacesetter notebook.

chapter 10

Master's Commission

Another Opportunity to Train the Saints

In recent years there has been a new level of leadership that has developed in many youth ministries across the nation. The program is called Master's Commission. There are several different styles demonstrated in these programs, but the thing that remains constant is the training of college-aged men and women via real ministry experience.

We began our Master's Commission program for Crossfire in 1993. The reason that I was anxious to start this style of leadership program was specifically because of frustration and concern. Within my first six months at Crossfire, I received several different phone calls from young youth ministers who were frustrated, confused, and complaining of being ill prepared for the ministries they were leading. But there was one statement that I continued to hear over and over again that simply broke my heart and caused me to want to create a solution: "Bret, I'm so confused. I'm not even sure if God really called me into ministry." These were young men and women who had done all they knew to do. They had accepted Christ as Savior, attended a youth group, went off to Bible college, completed their formal education, and accepted a position that they felt God had provided. And now, several months later, they were questioning their call! That didn't sound right to me. Something was missing.

> . . . the focal point must be on the development of young people, leadership, and ministry skills.

That something was the practical aspect of their training—practical training in outreaches, teaching, leading outings, working with a staff, how to balance family and ministry, and learning to stay strong with God while ministering full time. After years of leading a Master's Commission program, I have been delighted to see that the young people are prepared in a very real and practical way. Nothing can replace two years of working with a pastoral staff. They finish their time and training well prepared.

I believe in the Master's Commission program. But for it to be run correctly, the focal point must be on the development of young people, their leadership, and their ministry skills. If your goal changes from this, you and your intern will be frustrated. I have visited several different Master's Commission programs across the nation. I have seen some great programs and others that caused me some concern. If you are considering this type of program, or if you are leading this type of a program, here are ten essential guidelines.

1. Don't View the Interns as a Labor Force

Some of the internship programs that I have witnessed use young people as a labor force for the church.

That is not what this type of program is intended to accomplish. The focus has to be on investing into young lives. Now, I agree that young people need to learn how to serve and to develop a work ethic. No problem. But I do run into a problem when there is very little ministry opportunity, almost no leadership training, and no opportunity to make decisions. Interns will benefit you, your ministry, and your entire church if you give them half a chance. But remember, the blessing will flow from investing in them.

2. Your Goal Must Be to Give to Them

These young people have some real needs. Internship programs are designed to meet those needs. Please keep this as your focus. It makes me sad when interns are required to pay six thousand dollars per year to attend a program and then they are given very little in a personal way. The entire pastoral staff of the church should adopt the mindset of investing into these young lives. Anything less will result in a program that produces interns who are not prepared.

3. Don't Short Them on Formal Education

I am a believer in education. I believe with all my heart that God expects us to do all we can to equip ourselves for ministry. We need to do all we can so that we won't be limited when God decides to use us in ministry. Picture a tool belt. If you show up on a construction sight with no tools in your belt, you are of little benefit to the foreman of the overall project. But if you have a belt filled with tools and you know how to use them, you will be a valuable contributor to the project. So it is with us. We are responsible for filling our tool belt so that God can use us. Limited tools mean limited ability and opportunities.

Education is one of the tools that need to be placed in a young person's ministry tool belt. Every June, around graduation I hear this statement: "I don't need college. I just want to go and serve God now! People are dying and going to hell now. I can't afford to wait another four years." My heart beats with passion for the lost. I care about the work of God. But I understand that unprepared people are ineffective. If you run an internship program, please write formal education into your list of requirements. Too often, young people will go to an internship program for a year or two or possibly even three years. If they don't benefit from formal education during this time, they have put themselves behind everybody else who has been working on an education. Internships and education work together very naturally. Please make sure to include formal education in every internship program!

4. Give Them Real Ministry Opportunity

Service must be included in this, but if the only thing your interns are doing is cleaning, answering phones, and washing your car, then you are making a mistake. They need to experience the joys and trials of leadership. The only way they will learn to lead in ministry is for you to allow that to happen. Give them entire projects. Allow them to advertise, set the budget, recruit the workers, and lead the activity. Allow interns to experience the things that you view as viable ministry for your life. If you consider it real ministry for yourself, then allow them to try it!

5. This Program Is Not for Lazy Pastors

I have talked to many youth ministers who would love to start an internship program. One young pastor said, "I would love to have a couple of interns so that

I wouldn't have to work so hard. It would be great to give an intern some of the parts of ministry I don't like." Interns are not for lazy pastors! Interns represent extra work, time, energy, and money from you, Mr. Youth Pastor. *After* you have personally invested in them heavily, interns are a great asset to your ministry efforts. If your goal is to get two interns to make your life easier, do all of us a favor: Don't get the interns. You will be disappointed, and they will get hurt. There is no substitute for hard work in the ministry and no room for lazy ministers who want interns.

6. When They Succeed They Will Receive the Credit

This guideline was covered earlier, so I won't spend time covering the issue again. Suffice it to say, when people do the work, allow them to enjoy the credit. Taking credit for another's work only causes resentment and bitterness. Don't be selfish with the limelight. Allow your interns to enjoy success in their efforts.

7. Don't Let Them Be a Face in the Crowd

This concept becomes more difficult in larger programs, but it is still important. Each young person in your program comes from the factory equipped with strengths and weaknesses. They are individuals. They have individual needs and areas of concern. Don't let interns just become a face in the crowd.

The way I have been able to preserve this aspect of our program is two-fold. First of all, each intern is required to spend one half-hour with me each week. During this time, I turn my computer off, put the phone on DO NOT DISTURB, and then I simply listen to them. The time is designed for them to express themselves and their concerns. These meetings have proven to be some of the richest times I have had in ministry. Secondly, I require that each intern keep an interactive journal that is due each Friday afternoon. They are encouraged to write about their fears, joys, victories, and failures. I, in turn, write comments and encouragements back to them and return the journals by the first of the week. These times have helped me keep the individuality alive in a growing program.

8. The Youth Pastor Must Have Time for the Interns
This sounds a little obvious, but it needs to be stated. I recently talked to a young intern from another state that had just finished her first year of service. She was excited about all that God was doing in her walk with Christ but expressed disappointment in the fact that she never had the chance to converse with the director of the program. How tragic! Youth pastor, you must have time for your interns. There are many things that can be ignored, but an internship program is not one of them! Remember, people don't care how much you know until they know how much you care.

9. How Interns Must Be Viewed

- BY THE STAFF. An intern is veiwed as one who is learning about ministry, a student who is learning how to minister, a young person who is allowing God some time to speak to you about your life. Pastors who are willing to teach them and help them to acquire ministry skills like to see a teachable spirit, good attitude, and a consistent level of effort.
- BY THE CONGREGATION. Whether it's fair or not, interns are seen as an extension of the pastoral staff. In many situations, the congregation will hold them to the same level of expectations.

Interns will be watched on a constant basis. Their attitudes, appearance, and activities will be watched and will help the congregation determine the successes and failures of this style of program.

- BY THE YOUTH MINISTRY. Interns will be seen as absolute leaders. Personally, as the youth pastor, I work to establish each of my interns in their leadership roles. The youth ministry will watch interns' actions and imitate them. Parents and teens alike will view interns as role models. Interns minister in many settings more effectively than even the youth pastor can. They get to know people that the pastor may hardly know. Their success will be encouraged and backed by the youth ministry.

- BY THE YOUTH MINISTER. Interns are seen as ministers of the gospel to their local community. Youth pastors want interns to join them in effectively ministering to hurting teens who need Jesus. Pastors view interns as people with bright futures who are filled with promise.

10. You Must Be Willing to Make Each Intern Six Guarantees

GUARANTEE 1: QUESTIONS ARE ENCOURAGED

I make this guarantee to let the interns know they are in a safe learning environment. They have the right to ask me questions. Many young people are intimidated and will be shy on their own. But if you take time to make it a guarantee that you have time for their questions, then questions will be asked. As the questions are asked, the intern will grow.

GUARANTEE 2: YOU WILL BE STRETCHED

I love to make this guarantee to my interns. I tell them up front that I will learn what strengths and weaknesses they possess. I will help them to refine their strengths and exploit their weaknesses. I will help them with their weaknesses until those weaknesses become areas where they can perform with confidence and ability. If the intern hates being up in front of crowds, that's where I'll put them. If they don't like public speaking, they will speak in public. If they hate small group settings, they will lead a small group. Training, time, love, and investment will help stretch these young people until they become more than they ever thought possible. Stretch them!

GUARANTEE 3: YOU HAVE THE FREEDOM TO FAIL

Interns must be allowed to learn from their mistakes. The first step is to create a safe environment where they have the freedom to fail. As a result of this philosophy, my interns gave me the nickname The Crap Shield. It's not an overly spiritual title. Relax, it has a good meaning. I do everything I can to allow them to do their best in a free-to-fail environment. When they do fail, I never let the heat fall onto them. There are a lot of harsh aspects of ministry that interns simply aren't ready to handle. I protect them. I hold them accountable, teach them from their mistakes, and encourage them to try again. But I never allow the anger or blame to fall on one of my interns. They have the freedom to fail. I want them to try hard to do their best without the fear of getting into trouble with the pastor. They are my responsibility. I take the heat; they get to learn.

GUARANTEE 4: YOU MUST EARN RESPECT

This guarantee is one that you simply can't change. It is a fact of life and a fact of leadership. Respect is not handed out; it must be earned. Please take time to explain this to your interns. It will save much confusion and difficulty in the beginning of their internship time with you and your ministry.

GUARANTEE 5: I WILL BACK YOU

This is my personal promise that I believe in them, that I will stand by my intern even when they are wrong. It means that when people doubt them, I won't. When people want to badmouth an intern, I will be at their defense. When they are discouraged, I provide encouragement. Backing somebody means being there on a consistent basis, being supportive to the end, and committed to seeing the end result in the young intern's life. Youth pastor, back them.

GUARANTEE 6: IF THERE'S A PROBLEM, I WILL COME TO YOU

This guarantee promises open honesty and ensures a level of respect. I want my interns to spend time in ministry, not trying to figure out if I am upset with them about something. For this reason, I promise them I will come to them with problems. If they don't hear from me, then everything is OK. "If your brother sins against you, go and show him his fault, just between the two of you. If he listens to you, you have won your brother over" (Matthew 18:15). This is a scriptural principle that works as an effective guarantee for interns.

◊◊◊

These ten guidelines are essential for the success of a Master's Commission program. Anything less may be easier for you, but it will short the interns in experience and readiness for ministry. Please remember that the primary reason for this program is to provide you and your church staff the opportunity to invest into the lives of young, future ministers.

I want to share a few facts about running an internship program that must be understood before you start.

- Fact: There is only so much you can do by yourself. Interns enable you to do more of the ministry to which you were called.
- Fact: Real experiences are needed for your youth to succeed in ministry after they graduate from college.
- Fact: You can only grow to a certain point without training and equipping a staff to help you.
- Fact: Your interns will perform some aspects of ministry more effectively than you can. Let them succeed.
- Fact: Insecure youth pastors are ineffective with intern programs. Let them succeed. Let them look good. It's not about you; it's about them.
- Fact: You must learn to spend 80 percent of your time with 20 percent of your people. That 20 percent will, in turn, do the work of the ministry.
- Fact: Your job is to train and equip saints to do the work.

I believe the most powerful proof of the program's value is the interns themselves. I wish that you could spend an hour with each intern on my staff. You would be a richer person for it. They are incredible individuals. The following segment is five short testimonies from young people who are pursuing the call of God on their lives. They are just average youth, from an average church, and doing incredible things for the Lord.

SEAN LOMAX, AGE 19

The Master's Commission program has been the greatest and most life-changing experience I have ever had.

After knowing that I had a call on my life to be a missionary and to serve in the ministry, I knew that the Master's Commission was going to be the way that I started to fulfill the calling and learn how to minister in a practical, hands-on way. In the past year and a half, I have developed more leadership abilities and developed my walk with Christ more than ever before. I was only saved for about a year and a half before I joined the team, and it has brought me farther than I ever could have imagined. I knew that if I had gone to Bible college right away, that I would have never gained the hands-on ministry experience that I received here. Working side-by-side with great pastors has taught me more than any class could.

In Master's Commission, we have the freedom to fail. If we mess up, we know it will be OK. Every failure is something that we should always learn from. This allows you to make the mistakes now that you might possibly make later when you don't have any room for failure. The most important lesson that I have learned while doing Master's Commission is how to be a servant-leader. I have learned what kind of work it really takes to minister effectively to youth, and what Paul meant when he said, "Do nothing out of selfish ambition or vain conceit, but in humility consider others better than yourselves" (Philippians 2:3).

My work ethic has changed so much, and I have learned how to deal with a lot of things I would have never even considered a problem in my life before. I have learned how to balance my ministry time and the time with my family; how to deal with stress, budgets, deadlines, big projects, and also specific situations that can only be truly learned when you are in them yourself.

It has been the greatest privilege to be able to work alongside pastors and to see how they run their different ministries. I was really affected one day when our senior pastor was telling us his vision for our church and pouring out his heart to us. That is something that I knew I was privileged to hear, and I knew that most people never get to understand their pastor in that way. Seeing things like that and seeing the way the pastors handle difficulties and problems in a close-up way will definitely cause me to more effectively serve God in the future.

Pastor Bret has been willing to pour his life into us. He doesn't just share with us in the accomplishments he has made or great things he has done, but he is also willing to show us who he truly is by also sharing the things that he didn't do right the first time. His honesty to us is one thing that I have always appreciated. He is never artificial and never blows off a chance to put into our lives and to teach us a lesson.

One of the biggest ways that the Master's Commission has helped me was in the area of stress, worrying, and self-esteem. For a long time, I thought that what I did determined my self-worth. I believed the lie that if I didn't do well in ministry, then I wasn't good enough and that I didn't deserve a second chance. I was constantly worried about my own image. After being in Master's Commission for a few months, I was already reaching the point where I wanted to give up because I was burning myself out. I didn't want to deal with all the stress anymore, and because of this I was becoming ineffective. But at just the right time, Pastor Bret came along and encouraged and told me that I am really working with God, not just for Him, and not just for Pastor Bret or any other person. He also helped me to understand that what I do does not equate to who I am. This was a life lesson that I would not have learned by simply going to school. I would not have run into this problem until it was too late, and I might have given up on my call into ministry.

Through doing Master's Commission, I have been able to see more of God moving in my life than ever, and I have come to know more of the heart of God than I have ever thought possible. Doing the Master's Commission program has laid a solid foundation for my training in ministry. I know that as soon as I leave it, I will be able to face the challenges that will come my way as I strive to fulfill the calling that God has placed upon my heart. Seeing the power of God and His Spirit move in a ministry, and being allowed to take part in it, has changed me forever. The Master's Commission program has only confirmed over and over that the calling on my life is real, and I only want to serve and surrender my life more than I ever did before.

ABBY BLANKENSHIP, AGE 20

My name is Abby Blankenship. I am serving my third year on Master's Commission. I've known that God was calling me into the ministry since I was thirteen. At that time, I was shy, emotional, and a very hurt little girl. I had no self-esteem, let alone any leadership qualities. I was a follower, not a leader. Very few people believed in me or in the call I felt. Yet God frequently put on my heart that He had a special plan for me. That little bit of truth was all I had going for me.

I started coming to Crossfire when I was a sophomore in high school. I came from a small youth group that did very little. The ministry opportunities I received just being a member of Crossfire began to change who I was. I was in the drama and worship team. I was even leading a successful Christian club on my high-school campus. I was getting to do what I've always dreamed I would do: ministry.

I decided to apply for Master's my senior year. To my amazement, I was accepted. Someone actually believed enough in me that they were willing to take a risk and put me on their staff. I was just an average youth member. I sang on the worship team just like twenty other people did. However, God singled me out. I remember the day Pastor Bret had a meeting with my parents about Master's. My mother told Pastor Bret that she wasn't sure I could handle the position. Pastor Bret lovingly said, "You see her for who she is right now. I see her for who she will become." Pastor Bret saw potential in me and was determined to expose it.

My first year was very hard. I was scared of failure, my coworkers, the pastoral staff, and even Pastor Bret. I thought the only gift I had to offer God in ministry was my singing voice. I just automatically assumed that whatever I did on Master's would be related to music. I was quick to find out how wrong I was. I'll never forget when our worship leader left and I was not asked to take it over. I was devastated. You guessed it, I cried.

I thank God I didn't end up leading the worship team. I knew music. That meant that Pastor Bret had to put me someplace else where I could be stretched and learn something new. I know that God is calling me to do much more than just stick a microphone in my face and hum a cute little tune. I am called to touch lives and see people get saved. This mindset has helped me see the difference between using music as entertainment versus using it for ministry.

I also remember the first time I blew an assignment. Like I said before, I was afraid of failure. What I didn't understand was that when you think like a failure, you fail. You get what you expect. This was another mindset that was dramatically altered because of Master's Commission. Instead of telling me how stupid I was, Pastor Bret gave me another assignment. He told me I had the freedom to fail. On top of that, he would take the blame for my mistakes and show me how to do it right. When I did it right, he gave me the credit. He wouldn't give me a step-by-step manual on how to organize a progressive dinner or an outreach. He would give me ideas or hints and let me do it on my own. He did whatever he could to set me up for success.

Youth pastor, this philosophy is so vital to any internship program you may be thinking of instituting. If Pastor Bret just told me exactly what I was supposed to do, step-by-step, I would leave this program as a cookie-cut product of Pastor Bret Allen. He and I are not alike. I will always do certain things differently than he does. It doesn't mean I'm doing things wrong, it just means that I am doing them with my own personality and not with his. The freedom to fail helped me kill my fear of failure. I came into this program thinking I had to earn love, even from God. I now understand that God loves me just for who I am. I don't have to prove my value to Him or anyone else. It's just there. Under Pastor Bret, I was also given an opportunity to learn from my mistakes that I would have ended up making in my own ministry. Because of this, I am more prepared for whatever God calls me to.

Being a part of Master's Commission has confirmed God's call on my life. It has helped prepare me for ministry. Some of my coworkers are not called to the ministry. However, this program has still developed them into better men and women of God. It has also taught them valuable skills to take with them wherever they go. I know how to lead. I have learned to trust people. I have learned about several different skills and talents I possess. I have learned to be objective rather than let my emotions rule me. I have learned the kind of treatment I deserve and the kind I don't need to take. I have learned to be a leader and to be assertive. Most importantly, I have learned that God is far more interested in who I am in Him than what I do for Him. I can attribute all of these things and so much more to this program. I hope this helps you to see the value of establishing a Master's Commission and developing the gold that is hidden in your youth ministry.

BRIAN COMPTON, AGE 19

Master's Commission has benefited my life in many ways since I have begun to minister here in June of 1997. It is such a wonderful program, because while learning how to do practical ministry, I have also benefited from weekly leadership equipping and personal meetings with Pastor Bret Allen. The meetings with Pastor Bret have been totally beneficial for me because I have him for a half-hour a week to talk about personal problems, concerns, leadership issues, ministry issues, and being the person who God wants me to be.

The Master's Commission program has allowed me to participate in real-life ministry, while the pastoral staff of Calvary Temple Church has helped me develop into the man God wants me to be. In the last year and a half, I have been allowed to run and operate ministries while helping a vital part of the church accomplish what it needs to effectively minister to the generation of youth in this area. In turn, Pastor Bret and the rest of the pastoral staff of Calvary Temple Church have equipped me with valuable leadership training and practical ministry experience.

Since beginning ministry with Master's Commission, I have learned that ministry takes a lot of work, but what I produce is not as important as who I am. Because of all the time spent investing into my life, I know that ministry is about people—touching people with Jesus so they can go and do the same to other people. I was not selected for Master's Commission so I could become a person on a church workforce. I was selected so God could work in my life and develop me to effectively minister to the youth culture of America. I am even more excited to get into full-time ministry than I was before I started Master's Commission. I have never been more excited to do the work of the Lord and to grow in my relationship with Jesus and with the people that I minister to and with.

JOHN JACKSON, AGE 21

I entered Master's Commission directly out of high school at the age of 18. Quite honestly, when I began, I didn't have much to offer in the way of leadership or administrative abilities. I had grown up in a Christian home and had attended Christian school for most of my childhood, but I did not know how to effectively lead and disciple others in Christ.

Although I had minimal experience in leading, Pastor Bret saw the situation differently. My eyes begin to tear as I think of how he believed in me and began pouring himself into my life. He didn't see me as just another guy who grew up in the church. Instead, he saw the potential that God could use to do great things for Him.

As the program started, I was given tasks and projects in which I could gain experience in leading. However, I was not simply expected to just know how to do these things. Pastor Bret always had his office and ears open to any questions I had. He did not pressure me or take the project over; he just let me know that he was there if I needed help. Of course, I did need help, and he was patient to help me do it right.

From that point, my responsibilities as a Master's intern grew larger and larger. Soon, I was given care of certain ministries within Crossfire. God began to use me in a wonderful way to touch and impact the lives of young people in our area! Leading began to get more comfortable to me the more I experienced it. I had never been anxious to be in the front of the pack, but Master's allowed my confidence to blossom as I worked under the leading of Pastor Bret.

I can truly say that Master's Commission helped create two of the greatest years of my life. Master's taught me how to lead and be an effective influence in the lives of teens. Now, I serve as the junior-high director for Crossfire. But without the foundation of Master's Commission, I would not be equipped or prepared for the things I deal with each day. God truly used my time as a Master's intern to form me into a person that can effectively minister to young people that come my way. I thank God for the Master's program and for the investment Pastor Bret has made into my life.

MATTHEW BLANKENSHIP, AGE 19

The Master's Commission program has been one of the single greatest blessings in my life. Not only has my life been blessed as a Christian young man, but as a future minister as well. This internship has been more adequately preparing me for a life in the ministry for the last year and a half. I can say with the utmost of confidence that the Master's Commission is one of *the* best, if not the best, training and equipping program for young men and women who seek to serve the Lord with their lives.

Master's Commission has taught me how important it is to be a model to the people. I have found that you never really know how much people watch and follow you until you see your attitude and character traits duplicated and lived in those around you. "We live in a fishbowl," Pastor Bret tells me. As ministers and pacesetters for the youth of this generation, we will be closely watched as standards that teach teens how to live their lives.

This reality has taught me to live a God-centered life that sets a high-integrity, moral lesson to all who see me. So, because of this lifestyle, not only do I set a godly example in the lives of others, I live a better life as well. This is one of the greatest truths that I have been taught while in Master's Commission.

For so long, I can remember hearing that I needed a broken heart for the lost and for the many people that I will minister to. This way of thinking and living surpassed me for quite a while. I couldn't quite understand why it was so important or why I needed this passion for the lost in ministry. I had heard it said but didn't see the need for it in my life. This lifestyle also changed as I served in this program.

As I grew in the Lord as a minister to the teens of Contra Costa County, my heart began to undergo a drastic transformation. I found myself growing to love the many people that I ministered to every day of every week. I began to pray fervently for the multitude of lost souls for whom I could place a face. I began to cry for those whom I knew were lost and needed Jesus in their lives. I was growing to love people. A passion was developing within me to seek out and save the lost. An amazing transformation had taken place within me, and God was using me in ways he never could before, because my heart hadn't been ready.

I stand here today a changed and renewed man. The Master's Commission has taught me to be obedient to God's will and submit to His calling. There has been no better teacher of this than the practical experience of ministry and my intimacy with God that Master's Commission has allowed and taught me to have. Should you entrust your life to God in this way, He will change you. I promise!

HARLEY ALLEN, SENIOR PASTOR, CALVARY TEMPLE CHURCH

As I have watched this program develop over the past several years, I am more and more enthusiastic about it. Our goal was to allow young people the opportunity to experience real-life ministry responsibilities. I think we have done that very well. I have been delighted to observe growth and maturity in the lives of these young men and women.

Please know that I feel honored to pastor a church that financially supports such a program for future leaders.

The Master's Commission

Student Purpose

1. To provide an opportunity for the student to give one year of his or her life to the Lord in full-time service in their home church
2. To rebuild a bridge between high school and college, better preparing the student for future plans and assessment
3. To equip the student for ministry
4. To gain practical ministry experience as they *do* the work of the Lord
5. To teach the student how to work

Church Purpose

1. To be obedient in making disciples (Matthew 28:19–20)
2. To receive full-time/volunteer laborers for the harvest (Matthew 10:37–38)
3. The church will benefit with laborers for:

- King's Crew
- Illustrated sermons
- Human videos
- Convalescent
- The Spot
- Prayer ministry

- Rock Solid
- Worship
- Street drama
- SR. RIOT
- JR. RIOT
- Newsletter
- Video production
- Welcome Wagon
- Home groups
- Battle Cry
- Cross Training
- Choir
- Dance
- Altar workers
- 180 Program
- Big Brother/Sister

Daily Schedule

It is my hope that Master's Commission will be a growth experience for you. It is my goal to provide an atmosphere where you can learn and allow God to utilize your life. My commitment level to you is very high. I want to see you succeed. To help with your process, the following items will be included in your schedule.

1. Each Master's member will attend staff devotions in the conference room at 8:45 A.M. each morning Tuesday–Friday, Sunday at 8:30 A.M.
2. Each day, 8:00–8:30 A.M. is blocked out for your personal devotions. These times are vital, as they will determine your ability to minister in difficult times. These times are foundational and should be seen as a priority before anything else in your work schedule. It is mandatory that all Master's Commission meet in the sanctuary during this time.
3. Each morning, Master's will meet with Pastor Bret at 9:00 A.M. in the conference room for prayer and daily assignments.
4. Each week, we will have a staff meeting on Wednesday at 9:00 A.M. This is the best time to discuss projects, calendars, and frustration in specific situations. It is set aside to enable effective communication to flow between us.

5. Each Master's person will keep a dialogue journal. This journal will be interactive in nature and will be passed back and forth from Pastor Bret to the respective Master's person. This journal will enable you to express concerns and ask questions while at the same time eliminate staff reports that have been utilized in the past. Journals will be due each Friday before the end of the workday and will be given back Sunday A.M.

6. Each week you will have a half-hour of one-on-one time with Pastor Bret. This time is designed to increase communication and to ensure that busy schedules don't prevent Pastor Bret from being able to train and help you in areas you are concerned about.

7. There will be a one-hour leadership training session once a week. The time of this class will be on Wednesday after staff meeting. These times will prove to be helpful, usable, and valuable to you in the future.

8. Each month you will be assigned a piece of leadership-development material. It will contain a leadership concept to help you develop in your position. Each piece of material will require a written one-page response.

9. Class schedules are encouraged to run on the Tuesday and Thursday schedule. Make every effort to leave Monday, Wednesday, and Friday free from school obligations.

Standard Procedures and Guidelines

Then Jesus came and spoke to them saying, "All authority has been given to Me in heaven and on earth. Go, therefore, and make disciples of all the

Nations, baptizing them in the name of the Father and of the Son and of the Holy Spirit, teaching them to observe all the things I have commanded you; and lo, I am with you always, even to the end of the age." (Matthew 28:18–20)

Standard Procedures

1. Disciples are to be available for assignment or work six days and/or nights per week.
2. Monday is your day off. Regarding your day off, observe the following:
   a. If you are planning to go out of town for longer than your day off, please notify Pastor Bret at least four days in advance.
   b. Localized activities on your day off do not need prior approval. Any such approval is subject to cancellation if it is in the best interest of the disciple of Master's Commission ministry.
3. Prior approval is required to be excused from any daily sessions (i.e., sickness, special circumstances).
4. Disciples are not allowed to take leave from Master's schedule without prior approval.
5. Mandatory activities:
   a. Comply with MC no-dating policy, dress code, and other standing rules and guidelines.
   b. Be at the appointed place at the appointed time, or at a known location as the result of prior approval and/or assignment.
   c. Bring a change of clothes each day.
   d. Maintain your vehicle in good repair and clean inside and out.
6. Car repairs are *not* Master's Commission responsibility.

7. All reimbursement receipts must be turned in to Pastor Bret.

8. Paydays are on the 15th of each month.

Activity Guidelines

1. Be at least 30 minutes early for all activities, including morning prayer, all church services, daily classes, work schedules, and outreaches.

2. Because of frequent unpredictable changes in scheduling, be flexible. It is the call of our ministry to be available.

3. Be respectful and attentive to lecturers and guest speakers.

4. No roughhousing or horseplay. If you break it, you pay for it!

Master's Commission No-Dating Guidelines

Welcome to Master's Commission's most violated guideline.

The purpose of these guidelines is to *protect* and *strengthen* your discipleship relationship with the Lord. Strict observation of these guidelines is necessary to produce the kind of group unity that is required of Master's Commission. Godly male-female relationships are encouraged in Master's; however, there shall be *no* dating! *Dating* is construed as whenever a male and female demonstrate by work or action that a special couple relationship exists. These guidelines apply even if one of the parties is not a part of Master's Commission. The following will be accepted as evidence that such a special relationship does exist.

1. In group setting (i.e., church services, Master's daily routines, banquets, rallies, youth activities, etc.)

    a. Sitting together as a couple or setting yourselves apart from the rest of the group

    b. Engaging in prolonged or "intimate" conversations apart from the rest of the group

    c. Demonstrating a special attention to or affection for each other that is different from what is shown to others in the group

2. In one-on-one settings

    a. Riding together in/on a vehicle and not accompanied by a chaperon (i.e., fellow Master's Commissioner or an approved adult over 21)

    b. Bible study, scripture memory, or other such "learning" activities together

    c. Private meetings at the apartment of either party (even with adult of other Master's disciples present) or similar places

    d. Phone conversations that are consistently longer than five (5) minutes

    e. Following each other home after activities "to make sure they get home safely"

If there are any questions about these guidelines, or any part of them, please talk with your supervisor. This is going to be one of the most incredible years of your life. You are going to see Jesus work in your heart and through your life like never before. But only one thing will make this happen: Your focus must be 100 percent on Jesus Christ! It is important that during the next year, you do not allow anyone or anything to take your eyes off Jesus.

Sometimes it is easy to emotionally date without ever giving the physical signs of dating. We consider emotional dating just as distracting. We desire that each Master's Commission disciple set himself or herself apart for God. Basically, when you come to Master's Commission, you are saying to God: "Jesus, here's one year of my life with absolutely no distractions. Mold me and make me into your image. Use me like never before. I want to leave here with an intimacy that few in this world may find."

I hope that this is your prayer. Emotionally "date" Jesus while you are here. By stating these suggestions, we are not trying to be legalistic, but realistic. It is so easy to lose focus and emotionally become attached to someone else. Guard yourself.

Dress Guidelines

The dress guidelines for Master's Commission are very simple: Remember that you are a minister who represents Jesus Christ. Dress neatly and tastefully. The following guidelines are provided as reminders.

FOR MEN

- Sunday A.M.: white shirt, tie, dark slacks
- Office attire: slacks, ties, banded collar shirts
- Church or hospital: slacks, shirt with ties only
- Visitation: slacks and sport shirts
- High-school Bible studies or college campuses: nice jeans, sport shirts

FOR WOMEN

- Sunday A.M.: skirts or dresses (no shorter than 3 inches above the knee)
- Sunday P.M. and office attire: slacks/skirt and blouses
- Hospitals or visitation: nice slacks or dresses. No jeans
- High-school Bible studies or college campuses: slacks, nice jeans. No tank tops. If you have a question, ask for clarification

Remember that *everything* you do is done for the Lord. You are to be a living example of this.

Application for Admission

Master's Commission
4725 Evora Rd
Concord, CA 94520
(925) 458-9100

Type or Print All Items in Ink.
If additional space is needed to complete any question, please use an additional sheet of paper.

Name: _____
       Last   First   Middle

Permanent Address: _____
City: _____
State: _____ Zip: _____

Home Phone: (___)_____
Best time to call: _____

Previous Address: _____
City: _____
State: _____ Zip: _____

Personal

Sex: male ( ) female ( )
Birthdate: _____ / _____ / _____ Age: _____
           MM   DD   YY
Graduation date from high school/GED: _____
Are you a veteran? Yes ( ) No ( )
Birthplace city: _____
State/providence or country: _____
Are you a citizen of the United States? Yes ( ) No ( )
If no, country of citizenship: _____

Spiritual

Have you accepted Christ as your personal Savior? Yes ( ) No ( )
Have you been baptized in water? Yes ( ) No ( )
Have you had an Acts 2:4 experience? Yes ( ) No ( )

Do you attend church regularly? Yes ( ) No ( )
Are you a member? Yes ( ) No ( )
Home church and denomination: _____
Pastor's name: _____
Phone: (___) _____

Church address: _____
City: _____
State: _____ Zip: _____

Family

Name of your FATHER or guardian:

_____
Is he living? Yes ( ) No ( )
Address: _____
City: _____ State: _____ Zip: _____
Phone: (___) _____
Occupation: _____
Has he accepted Christ? Yes ( ) No ( )
Denomination preference: _____

Name of your MOTHER or guardian:

_____
Is she living? Yes ( ) No ( )
Address: _____
City: _____ State: _____ Zip: _____
Phone: (___) _____
Occupation: _____
Has she accepted Christ? Yes ( ) No ( )
Denomination preference: _____

Education

High school: _____
Dates attended: _____
Did you graduate? Yes ( ) No ( )
College: _____
Dates attended: _____
Did you graduate? Yes ( ) No ( )
Other school: _____
Dates Attended: _____
Did you graduate? Yes ( ) No ( )

Employment

Present Employer: _____

Address: _____

Dates (from): _____ (to): _____

Past Employer: _____

Address: _____

Dates (from): _____ (to): _____

Health

Have you ever used illegal drugs? Yes ( ) No ( )

If yes, date of last use: _____

If yes, explain: _____

Do you currently smoke? Yes ( ) No ( )

Do you currently drink alcoholic beverages? Yes ( ) No ( )

If in the past, give date last used:

Tobacco: _____

Alcohol: _____

Have you ever been arrested? Yes ( ) No ( )

If yes, explain_____

_____

Were you convicted? Yes ( ) No ( )

Please describe physical or emotional limitations. State any special attention or treatment required. _____

_____

Has your education/employment been disrupted for any period of time because of a physical problem or nervous disorder? Yes ( ) No ( )

Do you have any allergies? Yes ( ) No ( )

If yes, explain: _____

Miscellaneous

Do you own a vehicle (you must own upon entrance) Yes ( ) No ( )

Do you have insurance? Yes ( ) No ( )

117

What is your definition of a "servant"?

_____

_____

What is your definition of "professionalism"?

_____

_____

What will you do after Master's Commission?

_____

_____

Please use an additional **typed** sheet of paper to complete the following:

1.   Please describe your leadership experience.
2.   Please list your greatest strengths.
3.   Please list your greatest weaknesses.

How do your parents (family) feel about you coming into Master's Commission? _____

Include a recent photo of yourself. (It will not be returned.)

I have completed this application honestly with all known information and have read the selection of prospective candidates and agree to abide by the rules of the Master's Commission. I understand this is a limited ministry and I may or may not be accepted to work in it.

Signature: _____

Date: _____

Parent's signature (if you are under 18):

_____

chapter 11

Start Doing

Adult Leaders

Stop Stewing and Start Doing

First things first, adult leaders are a necessity if you want to develop a growing youth ministry that will impact teens in your community. Most youth pastors see the need for adult workers, but some are trying to run their programs without this level of leadership. Unfortunately, those youth pastors see adult leadership as a threat, an intimidation. Some youth pastors view adult leaders as a necessary evil in youth ministry, as if they have to permit adult supervision into the program.

These attitudes and mindsets must change. Bad attitudes and rebellion prevent blessings. Adult leaders will provide a stability and depth in youth ministry that can never be equaled without them. The age and experience of adults should never intimidate you; it can provide great strength to your whole program. However, training this level of leadership is no different than any other on your team. The youth pastor must be willing to spend time, energy, and resources to equip the adult leadership team. Without this investment, adult leadership will be ineffective and could prove counterproductive to your efforts. Once again, it all rises and falls on your leadership. You have the responsibility to train adults in effective ministry.

Before we go further on this topic, I believe that it is important to discuss the "why" of having an adult leadership team. The reason why you have this level in your leadership team will dramatically determine the level of their effectiveness. I have personally witnessed three incorrect reasons for why youth ministries feel they have a need for adult workers.

Keeping control and order in the weekly service is the youth pastor's responsibility.

1. Van Drivers

I have seen several youth ministries that allow adults to be involved in youth ministry simply to fill transportation needs. This allows the youth pastor to move his ministry to camps, retreats, and conventions. The problem here is that with nothing more to do than occasionally drive a van, the youth worker becomes bored and will quit. They must be involved in the heart of the youth ministry or they will feel used and disillusioned.

2. Discipline

Many youth ministers use the adult workers to help keep order in the weekly youth service. Keeping control and order in the weekly service is the youth pastor's responsibility. You are responsible for training your young people in how to behave in a worship service; it's only effective when it comes from the front. In seven years of working at Crossfire, I never had to remove one young person for disturbing the flow of the service. It is vital that you are direct, firm, and consistent when it comes to correcting this type of problem. Consistency will keep the group under control—and cause the newcomers to conform to the norm of your service.

Young people live in a world with no boundaries. They play on a field with no rules. Leadership, discipline, and order are void in their lives. The problem is that they need it desperately. This is a practical area, but one we must be willing to help within our ministries. It is unfair to ask adults to come into a youth service and be responsible for policing the youth. That is not ministry. It is, however, frustrating and thankless. Nobody will stay long to fulfill such an assignment.

Too many times, a youth pastor will have other adults handle discipline because he wants to remain popular with the teens. If popularity is your goal, I would like to suggest a career change. Youth ministry is not a popularity contest. Teens will love and respect you as you have love for them and prove yourself to be honest with them. They don't mind the boundaries; they want them. They will respect the boundaries when you are consistent and loving in your approach. Discipline is a must, but it is *your* job. Don't put that on your youth workers.

> **Discipline is a must, but it is your job. Don't put that on your youth workers.**

3. The "Big Event" Mentality

The third incorrect reason for having adult workers is found in the big-event mentality. Here is how it works.

A. FRUSTRATION

Frustration usually stems from a lack of ministry growth. This causes panic and a desperate search for solutions. Typically, solutions come in the form of a big event. So a power team or band or evangelist is brought in to work their magic and "fix" the youth ministry. The problem is that this is reactive, not pro-active. It's simply a knee-jerk reaction to a problem that needs much more serious attention.

B. WILD PROMOTION

The second step is to begin the wild promotion. Fundraising takes place. Raffle tickets are sold. Posters are hung. Radio announcements are paid for. Phone calls are made. Friends are invited. Schools are notified. Everything that can be done has been done. The hope is that the whole town will come and get saved. Then the youth group should grow.

C. ADULT BABYSITTERS NEEDED

Suddenly, the youth pastor realizes that, if all goes well, hundreds of kids will be on the church property in just a few short days. He also realizes that there is no way that one youth pastor can possibly handle the crowd that is anticipated. The solution? Adult workers. The call goes out for adults who will help in the youth ministry for this big event, to "baby-sit" the project and make sure it doesn't get out of control.

D. LOOK FOR PROSPECTS

Now the youth pastor begins a recruiting drive— talking to parents of the teens, asking friends in the church, even announcements in the church bulletin to locate the necessary adult workers. Very little discrimination, if any, is used. Bodies are needed!

E. NEW LEADERS ARE INTRODUCED

The youth pastor meets a certain level of success with his efforts and has commitments from several adults who agree to help with this big event. They are introduced the following Wednesday night as new youth leaders.

F. NO RESPONSIBILITY AND NO TRAINING

The day of the big event finally arrives. All the pieces to the puzzle are in place—many of them at the last minute. The youth pastor begins the event and releases his new adult workers into the sea of teenagers. Unfortunately, most of these workers are not equipped in any way to do youth ministry. At the end of the day, all is well. Many new youth came to the event and several were saved. The new adult workers were touched and motivated to serve in the youth ministry. The youth pastor is delighted. His event was a success and the adults loved it.

G. DISCOURAGEMENT

The following Wednesday night, the new adult leaders show up for the midweek service at 7:00 P.M. They come in and sit down with the rest of the youth group. Then, at the end, they stand up and leave with the rest of the youth group. This pattern repeats itself until the adult workers realize they have no idea what they are expected to do. A couple of weeks later, they begin to get discouraged, wondering what happened to all the excitement they experienced at the big event.

H. QUIT

Finally, the adult workers become so disillusioned with the youth ministry they quit. As they walk away, they have a bad taste in their mouths about the lack of organization, direction, and ministry that is present in their church's youth group.

You may think I have exaggerated this point just a bit, but I just hit the nail on the head. I have witnessed this series of events over and over again. Ineffective adult workers are the result of an ineffective youth pastor. Adults must be trained, equipped, and shown what they are to do as a youth worker.

My personal reasons for building an adult staff differ greatly from the three I just discussed. I see the adult portion of my leadership team as an incredibly valuable piece to the overall puzzle. They can do things that make my ministry extremely effective, like showing youth things that simply can't be taught in a sermon. I value the adult leaders in Crossfire because they are servant-leaders. Their job description starts and ends on one single point: They are there to serve the youth. With this mindset, all of their ministries will bring about success. Youth ministry isn't about meeting your needs or meeting the needs of adult workers. It's about meeting the needs of the youth that come to your ministry. It's not about you; it's about them! Servanthood is the key to effective adult leaders. Servant-leadership is not an inborn quality; it must be taught.

> **It's about meeting the needs of youth that come to your ministry.**

Each one of my fifty-six youth workers are engaged in ministry responsibilities at our Thursday night service. Those ministries are service motivated. After the service, it is not unusual to see adults picking up paper or other trash, praying with a youth at the altar, giving rides home, helping in the café, or giving change for a phone call. They are active in serving our youth.

During the service, each adult worker operates as a "row pastor." Our youth room has thirty-two rows of chairs. Two adults are assigned to each row. Youth ministry is about meeting the needs of teens, and that is exactly what this program does. Instead of me being responsible for 600 youth on Thursday night, each set of row pastors takes care of twelve youth. Their job is to greet, welcome, and minister to the youth that may be sitting in their row that night. By doing this, I have insured two important things:

1. The needs of the youth have a chance to be met.
2. Every adult worker has an opportunity for real ministry.

Each night, just before worship, we stop the service and allow the row pastors five minutes to minister practical servanthood to their youth. These five minutes literally make a difference in young people's lives. For many, it is just what is needed to tear down walls of resistance so that Christ can change their heart.

> **The average adult in the midst of teens will insist upon being shown unearned respect . . .**

Servanthood! That is what transforms an adult into a youth worker. It is not born; it must be developed.

The average adult in the midst of teens will insist upon being shown unearned respect and admiration simply because they are older, more experienced at life, and have a head filled with gray hairs. The average adult will make statements like, "You have to listen to me. I'm older than you are! As a matter of fact, I'm old enough to be your parent!" There isn't a thirteen-year-old alive today that will respond well to that attitude. They simply will not respect a person with that kind of mentality.

Remember, leadership is influence. Leadership has nothing to do with your age, experience, gray hair, or ability to nag. It is all about influence. The only way I know to influence teens in this day and age is to serve them with a pure heart. Servanthood will afford you the opportunities to speak into the lives of teens. This is the solitary reason that my adult leadership team is on the bottom of my leadership flow chart. Their position is under the junior high, senior high, and Master's Commission because they are present to serve these young people.

> **The only way I know to influence teens in this day and age is to serve them with a pure heart.**

> Your attitude should be the same as that of Christ Jesus: Who, being in very nature God, did not consider equality with God something to be grasped, but made himself nothing, taking the very nature of a servant, being made in human likeness. And being found in appearance as a man, he humbled himself and became obedient to death—even death on a cross! (Philippians 2:5–8)

So how do I get quality youth workers like this? The answer is so simple many of you will reject it. To get great youth workers, you must make them. Great youth workers don't grow on trees or come parcel post from heaven. They are a product of leadership. Allow me to share the steps I take in selecting adult youth leadership.

1. THE FIRST ASSIGNMENT

When a new person comes to me and inquires about youth work, I always schedule a meal or meeting to discuss our youth ministry. During this meeting, I explain the purpose, vision, and mission statements of our youth ministry. I then give the interested person an assignment. I ask them to attend a midweek service, a Sunday morning class with the high school or junior high, and to attend an outreach into the community on a Saturday. I then tell them the reason for this request: "I want you to come and experience our ministry. I want you to see what we do here. I am excited about you if you are coming to help. But if you are coming in to change things or straighten me out, I want to tell you up front that it won't work. God has called me to be the youth pastor. He has given me the vision for this ministry. I am not looking to have an adult worker attempt to change the direction God has called us to."

With that said, I ask them to complete the assignment and then set a follow-up meeting with me. I can already hear the objections. "Man, that sounds a little hard." No, it's just being honest. I am not looking for trouble. I tell my leadership that before they even start. For that reason, we have never had a major problem within our adult leadership ranks.

2. THE PROBATION

After the three-part assignment, 50 percent never contact me again. That is good, because I have successfully proven something: Not everybody is intended for youth ministry. I have eliminated 50 percent of problems from ever occurring. Standards and honesty have a way of doing that! For the 50 percent that return for our second meeting, I place them on a six-month probation within the youth ministry. They are assigned to another youth worker but hold no real authority until the six months are over. Six months? Isn't that a long time? Yes, but it takes time to produce quality in an adult worker. It will take a youth worker six months to learn our way of ministering, to understand our philosophies, and to know who I am as the youth pastor. This time makes all the difference in the longevity of a youth worker.

Another reason that I insist upon six months is that most people I have known can hold up a façade about themselves for a month or two, even three months if they are accomplished at the art of deception. But I have never met anyone who can hold up a façade for six whole months. At the end of six months I will know who they are. I will know if they possess the all-important ministry trait of consistency. I will know if I want them influencing my youth ministry or not. Six months sounds like a long time, but it really isn't when you consider how important the task is that surrounds the adult worker: serving youth who need to accurately see the love of Christ!

3.   APPLICATION AND FINGERPRINTING

This is the final step before allowing an adult to join my staff. I have them fill out a four-page application. (A copy is included at the end of this chapter.) I also ask that they go down to the police department and get fingerprinted. The fingerprint card is then handed in along with the completed application. I turn the information into our business manager and have a complete background check performed. This is to ensure that my youth workers aren't criminals, child molesters, or pedophiles.

4. TRAINING

After they are accepted as an official youth worker, and following six months of probation, they are announced and introduced to the

> **I have never met anyone who can hold up a façade for six whole months.**

entire youth ministry in a Thursday night service. It is a festive atmosphere. Everybody knows the commitment that has been required to reach this level. From this point on, each adult leader is required to attend monthly leadership training. I hold the classes on Sunday afternoons before the evening service. They are ninety minutes in length, and we discuss how to be better servant leaders.

Adult youth workers are a blessing from God! They will enrich your life and your ministry efforts incredibly, but only if they are recruited and trained correctly. Nothing in this world will speak louder to a troubled teen than an adult who is willing to serve them and share the love of Jesus week after week in real, practical ways.

Qualifications for Christian Education Workers

Christians who are in places of responsibility in the church are required to be examples in faith, conduct, and business affairs. To maintain a high standard for workers is one of the best ways to present Christ to the people of our community. Therefore, the following guidelines will be required of any person who works in the Christian Education Ministry at Calvary Temple Church.

1. Agree with the tenets of faith of Calvary Temple Church.
2. Make a minimum six-month commitment.
3. Complete a Christian Education Worker Application.
4. Be loyal to the pastor and leaders of Calvary Temple Church.
5. Be faithful to your assigned position.
6. Attend all workers' meeting and workshops.
7. Be faithful to attend regular church services.
8. Give at least three (3) days notice if you know you will be absent.
9. Be at your designated post fifteen (15) minutes before starting time.
10. Be neat in your appearance.
11. Keep your home life in order.
12. Give thirty-days (30) notice when resigning position.

Please read and sign.

I have read the above qualifications and pledge to keep them to the very best of my ability. I clearly understand that failure to keep any of the above qualifications is grounds for dismissal.

Signature: _____

Date: _____

Confidential
Christian Education Worker Application

This application is to be completed by all applicants for any position (volunteer or compensated) involving the supervision or custody of minors. It is being used to help the church provide a safe and secure environment for those children who participate in our programs and use our facilities.

Date: _____
Name: _____
Address: _____
City: _____
State: _____ Zip Code: _____ Phone: (___)_____
Male ( ) Female ( )
Birthdate: ____ / ____ / ____ Marital status: _____
Spouse's name (if married): _____
Maiden name: _____
Anniversary date (if married): _____
Will your spouse be involved in children's ministry? Yes ( ) No ( )
Number of children: _____
Your SSN(s), present and past: _____
Spouse's SSN(s), present and past: _____
Alias (other names): _____
_____

Present employer: _____
Can we call you at work? Yes ( ) No ( )
Work phone: (___)_____
Are you a member of Calvary Temple? _____
How long have you attended Calvary Temple? _____
Are you born again? Yes ( ) No ( )
Where did that occur? _____
Year: _____
Have you been baptized in water? Yes ( ) No ( )
If yes, where did that occur? _____
Do you tithe on a regular basis to Calvary Temple? Yes ( ) No ( )

Do You Believe . . .
[Yes] [No]
___ ___ in the virgin birth and deity of our Lord Jesus Christ?
___ ___ that Jesus is God's son and the only sacrifice for sin?
___ ___ that man must be born again to receive eternal life?
___ ___ in eternal reward for the believer? (Heaven)

____ ____ in eternal damnation for the lost? (Hell)
____ ____ in the infallibility of Scripture?
____ ____ that divine healing is part of redemption's purchase and is God's will for all who believe?
____ ____ that Jesus arose bodily from the dead?
____ ____ in the infilling of the Holy Spirit?
____ ____ that speaking in tongues is the initial evidence of the Baptism of the Holy Spirit?

Worker Application

List (names and address) of other churches you have attended regularly during the past five (5) years:

_____
_____
_____

List any gifts, callings, training, education, or other factors that have prepared you for children's/youth ministry: _____

_____

Have you ever led a child to Christ? Yes ( ) No ( )
Have you ever helped a child receive the Holy Spirit? Yes ( ) No ( )
Have you ever been involved in children's/youth ministry before? Yes ( ) No ( )
If yes, in what areas?

_____

With what church or organization?

_____

Do you have any physical handicaps or conditions preventing you from performing certain types of activities relating to youth or children's work? Yes ( ) No ( )
If yes, please explain:

_____
_____
_____

Have you been involved in homosexual activity within the last five (5) years? Yes ( ) No ( )
Do you presently have any communicable diseases (including HIV or AIDS)? Yes ( ) No ( )
If yes, please explain:

_____
_____

Do you smoke? Yes ( ) No ( )
Do you drink? Yes ( ) No ( )
Do you use illegal drugs? Yes ( ) No ( )
Why do you want to be involved in children's ministry?

_____

Indicate Areas of Interest

___Teach in class	___Storytelling	___Food services
___Art	___Musical Instrument	___Bulletin board
___Crafts	___Bus worker	___Office skills
___Help in class	___Flannelgraph	___Painting
___Carpentry	___Praise & worship	___Intercessory prayer
___Audio/media	___Bus visitation	___Costume clowns
___Puppet team	___Object lessons	___Children's choirs
___Outreach	___Writing skits	___Easter Saturday
___Games	___Bus driver	___Ushers
___Sewing	___Drama	___Greeters
___Electrical	___Publications	

___Harvest party

What age group do you desire to work with, and which day?

___Nursery	___Sunday
___1 & 2's	___Wednesday
___3–K	___Thursday
___Grades 1–5	___Friday
___Bus ministry	___Saturday
___The Spot	

Which weekend service do you attend? _____
What service would you be able to work in? _____
Is your spouse and/or family in agreement with you working in the
    Children's Department? Yes ( ) No ( )

Personal References
(Not employees or relatives)

Name: _____
Address: _____
Phone: (_____)_____

Name: _____

Address: _____

Phone: (_____)_____

Pastoral Reference

(Former senior pastor, associate pastor, or ministerial supervisor.)

Name: _____

Address: _____

Telephone: _____

Applicant's Statement

The answers given by me to the foregoing questions and the statements made by me are complete and true to the best of my knowledge and belief. I understand that any false information, omissions, or representation of facts called for in this application may result in rejection of my application or discharge from any assigned duties at any time during my service at Calvary Temple Church. I authorize Calvary Temple Church and/or its agents to verify any of this information, including, but not limited to, criminal history and motor vehicle driving records. I release all persons, schools, companies, churches, and law enforcement authorities from any damage whatsoever for issuing this information. I further waive any right to inspect information provided by the above sources on my behalf.

Should my application be accepted, I agree to be bound by the constitution, bylaws and policies of Calvary Temple Church, and to refrain from unscriptural conduct in the performance of my services on behalf of the church.

Applicant's signature:

_____

Date: _____

Witness:

_____

Date: _____

Accurately Measuring Youth Ministry Success

A friend of mine once told me, "Bret, the day that you begin to believe what people are saying about you, that is the day you are really in trouble." I've thought a lot about that statement over the years that I've been involved in youth ministry. I've come to the conclusion that it is, without a doubt, true. There have been times when people have criticized my best effort, questioned my ability, or doubted my call to ministry. They even have played God in my life, telling me where I should and where I should not minister. Listening to them would have been tragic. The day you honestly believe what people say about you—good or bad—you are in trouble.

On the other side of this issue are the people who have had a positive opinion of my ministry. Their comments are just as incorrect because they only see my accomplishments and my achievements. They simply miss, or choose to overlook, my faults and failures. The statements they make are kind and filled with praises, but they don't paint an accurate picture. If I were to buy into these opinions about my ministry, it would be just as destructive. Having said that, I think we can all agree that people's opinions are not a good gauge for measuring the success of your ministry. People's opinions change with the wind. You can never determine the success of your ministry by what people think or by what people say. Most of the people in your life are in no position to pass judgment on your ministry, because they have no understanding of what an effective youth ministry is.

> **The day you honestly believe what people say about you—good or bad—you are in trouble.**

Now, I understand how easy it is to say this and how hard it is to live it every day. The old adage is, "Sticks and stones will break my bones, but words will never hurt me." Nothing could be further from the truth. Words do hurt. When they are hurled at the wrong time, when you are down and hurting, they can hit like a fist. I have adopted a rule for my life concerning critics. Simply stated, "Unless you have walked with me, prayed with me, worked with me, and cried with me for six months, you have not earned the right to criticize me. After six months of serving with me, I will listen to you." People's opinions are not an accurate gauge for your life and ministry.

I believe that the only way to accurately measure true success in your ministry is by looking at how effective your youth group members prove to be in the future. When the teens who are currently in your youth ministry become ministers, then we will know how successful you were.

Recently, a fellow youth pastor said to me, "You are successful in your ministry. I would love to have your level of success."

The words sounded nice; they made me feel good. But my answer brought about a long period of silence, "We won't know if I have been successful for another twenty years. That is when we will all know how well my youth are doing in their ministries." My calling is to equip the saints to do the work of ministry. That means I should be producing people who can do the work of the ministry. It only stands to reason that my success rises and falls on this point. Attendance numbers don't tell the whole story. Magazine articles don't tell the whole story. People and their opinions aren't always accurate. But ministry results never lie. The fruit will tell the whole story.

I expect to see great things from the young people who have grown up in Crossfire. I believe they will shape future ministries in a dramatic manner. They have something that gives them an opportunity to do greater things than my ministry has ever accomplished: They have a starting point that is far superior to the one I started on. The youth group that I attended in Washington State had twelve students. To say that it was dry and lifeless would be a major compliment. I never invited friends—I was too embarrassed. When I recommended ideas, they were ignored. Even our trips and

> **After six months of serving with me, I will listen to you.**

activities demonstrated very little imagination. This is what I considered normal and acceptable. But it is totally different for the youth in Crossfire. They enjoy an atmosphere where they are encouraged to lead, grow, and try new things. They see what we are doing as normal. That is where their ministry ideas will begin, and it's a great place to start. When they push and stretch themselves and their ministries, their success will be the true measure of my success.

To ensure that the future is bright for these young ministers of the gospel, I have seven promises to them and their future ministries. I first heard these promises from Dr. John Maxwell, and I quickly adopted them for my ministry and those I minister to.

My Seven Promises to My Youth Ministry
The Next Generation

PROMISE 1: I PROMISE TO BELIEVE IN YOU

Powerful words combined with action cause lives and futures to be changed. People will rise to the level of expectation that you set for them. I want to be one who goes on record for believing in this generation. I want to be known as a pastor who believed not in word alone, but in my actions. I promise to be a pastor who consistently sets high expectations and helps you meet them.

PROMISE 2: I PROMISE TO PAVE THE WAY FOR YOU

It is my hope that the next generation of ministers will benefit from my learning and example. It is my hope that the ministries you lead will far exceed the things that we have done together. It is my honest hope that the student will be greater than the teacher.

PROMISE 3: I PROMISE TO HAND THE BATON OFF TO YOU

The day will come when I have aged and slowed. At that time, you will come running in behind me. I promise to hand the baton off to you and then cheer for you as you pass me by. I promise to be your greatest fan, because I believe in you!

PROMISE 4: I PROMISE TO POINT TO YOU

I promise to feature you, to allow you to step into the limelight. I promise to help you succeed. And when you do, I will allow you to get the credit and enjoy the success of your efforts.

PROMISE 5: I PROMISE TO PRAY FOR YOU

I promise to be a constant prayer support for you. I commit myself to be concerned about you, your family, and your ministry, so that I can effectively lift you before the Lord.

PROMISE 6: I PROMISE TO BLESS YOU

I promise that I will be there to put my arm around your shoulder and bless you both physically and spiritually to the best of my ability. I have put my life into yours. Please know that I wish for that type of relationship to continue.

PROMISE 7: I PROMISE TO LOVE YOU

I promise to be committed to the success of your ministry. I will strive to be a constant in your life. I will love you and be there for you, as you need me.

Success

True success can only be measured in terms of what fruit comes from the lives and ministries that you have invested in. I encourage you to remember this as you work in your youth ministry: You are shaping ministers. You are equipping those who will do the work. Make a commitment to them and to their ministries. Concern yourself with their success. *Then* you will be truly successful.

Appendix

Serious Tools for Youth Ministry Leadership

Manuals

The SPOT ("how-to" w/ video) $40
> Start your own Spot. Interesting tips on creating exciting teen out-
> reaches.

Master's Commission $25
> Start your own internship program and train young people to minister
> effectively.

VIPs: Visitation and Follow-Up $25
> Make sure your midweek visitors are taken care of. Show them that they
> are the VIPs in your ministry.

U-Turn Discipleship $12
> This effective five-week discipleship program includes five teacher's les-
> sons and five blank student lessons.

Illustrated Sermons

Blockades on the Road to Hell $30
> God doesn't send people to hell. The roadblocks are there, so going to hell
> requires real effort. This powerful evangelism tool will grip your audience.
> (Actors: 2–25)

Blood Bath $30

What is the biblical truth about the blood of Jesus and how to find forgiveness and enter heaven? Satan has changed our perpective on blood. (Actors: 3–50)

Choices $30

We are responsible for the decisions we make. This humorous yet tough look at freedom of choice and its consequences will knock people off the fence. (Actors: 10–50)

Dead End $30

Set in a concentration camp, this message of surrender and sacrifice makes teens the prisoners. Some are dragged off by soldiers and killed. The entire group is encouraged to lay their lives down for Christ. (Actors: 5–35)

Deep Impact $30

While Christians on a dock are preoccupied with church life at the water's edge, the water is full of the drowning lost. (Actors: 8–25)

Electric Chair $30

If Jesus were to have walked on earth today, how would he have reacted to our problems? And if He was sentenced to death in the electric chair, would you wear one around your neck? (Actors: 15–75)

The Empire Strikes Back $30

God created man for fellowship. Satan tried to destroy it. See each deliberate step, and how God strikes back to reunite us with Him. (Actors: 5–50)

First and Goal $30

Two football teams, Crusaders and Hades Destroyers, show how Christians must be wise to reach the goal. The Holy Spirit is our frontline of protection. Perfect for Superbowl events. (Actors: 10–100)

The Good, the Bad, and the Ugly $30

Audiences cheer about ridding themselves of the works of the flesh? Based on Ephesians 5, the works of the flesh and the spirit are shown in dramatic form through two humorous dramas. (Actors: 1–10)

Good Ol' Sam $30

This modern-day Good Samaritan parable will challenge and minister to any group. (Actors: 2–25)

Knock, Knock $30

Who's there? Christ, waiting to change your life. In an overview of the whole Bible, from Genesis to Revelation, Jesus is obviously the door. (Actors: 15–100)

Life Stinks $30
Similar to *It's a Wonderful Life*, examine what life would be like if the Cross never happened. Great evangelism. (Actors: 2–10)

Now What? $30
It's after the rapture, and the audience has been left behind. Who is ready? Powerful ending. (Actors: 5–50)

Outbreak $30
Sin is the plague of all time, but a cure is available. (Actors: 10–50)

To Hell and Back $30
An in-your-face tour of hell, with Satan as your guide. Lies and schemes are exposed, and Jesus is triumphant. (Actors: 15–100)

The Trial $30
On trial before God, with Satan as prosecutor, witnesses reveal that the the speaker stands guilty. A touching conclusion reveals Jesus as the perfect advocate. (Actors: 5–25)

The Ultimate Scarecrow $30
Keep your group riveted as they unmask the scarecrow, who is keeping them from the good stuff Jesus has: salvation, healing, and the Holy Spirit. (Actors: 1–20)

The Wall $30
If we're not careful, the enemy can sneak in through laziness, anger, selfishness, and more to tear down our wall. God is the only one who can repair us. (Actors: 8–20)

Who Cares? $30
Young people will be shocked by the stories of people who have laid down their lives to show they care. Here is hope for a generation. (Actors: 10–50)

Order Today
1. Shipping & Handling: Add 15% to total.
2. Make checks payable to:

Bret Allen
PO Box 276461
Sacramento, CA 95827

Questions? (209) 745-3401 or resources@toolzone4leaders.com

Serious Tools
for
Serious Leaders

ToolZone 4 Leaders is a new resource for youth leaders that delivers confident and effective training tools, including top quality books, videos, tapes, and how-to manuals.

Charisma magazine has acknowledged Executive Director Bret Allen for his success in building strong youth groups. Pastor Allen is helping to support and train over 400 youth leaders in Northern California and Nevada. Bret's pace is vigorous, his style is direct, his methods challenging, and his heart is aimed at encouraging and equipping leaders to succeed.

(209) 745-3401
www.toolzone4leaders.com